Fallen Passion Uncut
Author: Pamela Farmer
ISBN 978-0-61515519-7
Copyright 2007
ALL Rights Reserved
Publisher: Pamela Farmer

Rules of Service

If you sing, don't testify.
If you testify, don't sing.
Remember, you can't tell it all,
So don't even try.
And by all means,
Remember your Brothers and your Sisters.

What Beauty!

What beauty is there for you to see,
In my soul, the place called 'me!'
Not the me that I once was,
But the me that I now be-
Once so fragile and ashamed,
I now walk in victory!

What beauty is there for you to find,
Written on the pages of my mental maze!
No longer tucked in a secret place,
No longer hidden by disgrace.
The mask of sin is gone at last,
Finally, I can show my face.

What beauty lies in this heart of mine!
Come closer. Look deeper. You're sure to find,
A hidden treasure of the rarest kind,
It will surely blow your mind!

View my soul. Ponder my past. Can you see
That the hand of God was and is on me?
Of course you can! Now bask in His glory,
As you ponder your own story.
Look in the mirror, say; "I'm finally, free!
Thank you, God! It's really me!
I truly can now see!
Glory in the highest! What beauty!"
ME!

Prologue

She picked up the phone and dialed his number. His phone rang.

"Hello," the answer came in a thick Nigerian accent.

"Hi."

"Evette? Is that you?"

"Yeah."

"What's wrong?"

"I called to apologize to you for my behavior today on the phone. I'm sorry. You didn't deserve that. We were in the middle of an argument when you called and…well, I'm sorry."

"You have nothing to apologize for. I wasn't offended. Anyway, I was just kidding with what I said." There was a pause. "Are you crying?"

"Yes."

"You sound funny. What are you doing?"

"I'm getting drunk off the wine you brought on Sunday for dinner."

"Why are you crying and getting drunk? Where are your husband and your children?"

"Alexander is at work. The kids are playing and are about to go to bed."

"So why are you hurting yourself?"

"Because I'm tired."

"Tired of what?"

"Everything." She broke down. The tears began to pour like streams of water from a broken dam, and she opened herself up to him. "I'm tired of being neglected. I'm tired of being unappreciated and taken for granted. I'm tired of being the main source of income for this family…"

He interrupted. "I didn't know things were that bad. I was under the impression that you and your husband had the ideal marriage."

"You were able to think that only because I'm a good actress and I've grown accustomed to wearing a mask in public."

"Do you wanna talk about it?"

"Not with you."

"Why?"

"Because I'm a Christian and you're an atheist. That's why."

"Like I told you at work, an atheist is the best person for a Christian to talk to because you don't have to worry about information that's one-sided, nor do you have to worry about being indoctrinated. All I could do is offer you a fresh perspective."

"Well, alright. It started when we were first married. The first 2-½ months were bliss. Then one of his brothers came to our home, beat me and tried to rape me. Things have been down hill since then because I haven't been able to let it go. I mean, he didn't do *anything*. I would have at least felt better if he'd yelled at him, but he didn't even do that."

She continued. "Last year, we lost our house, our car. He filed bankruptcy, now I have no choice but to do it too before they come after me. My family is so disgusted until they told me they won't do another thing to help me unless I leave him and take the children with me."

He quietly listened as she went on about how her father owns his own company in Nevada and promised to buy her a house out there and said she could work for the company. Her aunt in Maine promised her a job as Assistant Manager of one of the apartment complexes that she over sees and told her she could live there rent-free. Martha told her that the last things she'd ever have to worry about are where she's going to live and work. All she had to do was leave her husband.

He sighed. "My heart goes out for you. If you would please forgive me for saying this, but your husband is a moron."

"If he's a moron, what does that make me? After all, I did marry him."

"That makes you human." He heard her sigh. "Are you alright? How much have you consumed so far?"

"Almost the entire bottle. I'm feeling pretty mellowed out right about now."

"Can I ask you a question?"

"Sure, anything you like. Doesn't mean I have to answer it, though."

"What is it that you want from your husband?"

She took a deep breath and let it out slowly. "I want him to appreciate me and the things I do. I want him to make me feel special." She began to cry a bit. "I want him to make love to me. To take his time and make love to me. Make me into a sundae. Put whip cream all over me and take his time licking and sucking it off. I want him to savor me. To talk to me sometimes. He can start there."

"I wish I was there to hold you right now."

She was startled by his confession but since he was being open, she decided to do so as well. "To be honest with you, I wish you were here to hold me, too."

"You lie."

"No. I've been attracted to you for months. I've been dreaming about you for weeks now, every night."

This time she heard him sigh. "What are you doing?"

He ignored her question. "Can you do me a favor?" he asked.

"Sure. Anything."

"Can you caress yourself for me?"

She did and sighed. She couldn't believe how wet she was just from hearing the
sound of his voice.

"Now, stick your fingers inside you."

She did, and sighed again. Then she sucked her juices from her fingers. He heard the sound and asked, "What was that?"

She said, "Oh, I just tasted myself, that's all."

He sighed heavily. "How do you taste?"

"Sweet."

Another heavy sigh and he said, "I'll be there in ten minutes."

"Are you crazy? There is no way I'm going to let you come in here and screw me in my husband's bed with my kids here. No way."

He suggested his car. She told him she wasn't some high school girl or college freshman.

"Is it because you're drunk?"

"No. I believe people use alcohol and drugs as scapegoats for having said or done what they always wanted to. I've never been so drunk that I did or said anything unwittingly. If I say it or do it, it's because I always wanted to. I think people should stop blaming their behavior on substances. If I screw you at all, it will be because I've wanted to for a while anyway, not because I'm inebriated. O.K.?"

"What are your children doing now?"

"They are asleep."

"Can I come?"

"No."

"Please. I want you so badly. I want to hold you, to feel you, to comfort you. I've desired you for a while also. You're so beautiful and your eyes, they're just exquisite. I'm so hard. Can I come?"

"Yes."

He was shocked. "You won't change your mind when I get there will you?"

"No."

"Promise?"

"I promise."

"I'll be there in ten minutes."

"I'll be waiting outside."

As drunk as she was, she ran into the bathroom, plugged in the curlers and hopped in the shower. Then she bumped a few curls in her hair, brushed her teeth, put Elizabeth Arden's *Splendor* scented lotion all over her body and hopped in a silk negligee. She threw on a long, black trench coat, got the White Zinfandel wine bottle and waited for him outside. The children were in their beds knocked out for the night. She saw the lights of his burgundy Camaro turn into the parking lot and smiled.

He met her half way and when they were face-to-face, he grabbed her waist, pulled her to him and stuck his tongue in her mouth. She responded and they were off. She'd almost slipped getting into the car, but his strength bore her up. When they began to drive off, they glanced at each other with anticipation and smiled. He stuck his fingers up her vagina and she rotated her hips with pleasure. Then he sucked her juices from his fingers and caressed her cheek with his hand. He grasped her left hand and placed it on his penis. He was as hard as a rock, and in her mind, he seemed to have a length that went on forever.

Within minutes they were at his place. It was your typical Baltimore brownstone. He told her that one of his cousins owned it and rented it out to members of the family. He lived on the third floor, a female cousin lived on the second floor and another cousin and his wife and kids lived on the first floor. He turned the alarm off and they quietly tipped up the stairs. He'd left the television on BET and all the lights were off – only the television lit the room.

He took the wine from her and sat it on the table. Then he turned and stared her in the eyes. For a few moments, they were suspended in time. He unzipped her coat and smiled as he saw what she was wearing; a whit, silk negligee with wine colored flowers trimmed in gold. "Nice." He said and then proceeded to quickly remove it.

He held her so tightly and kissed her so passionately. It was almost as if he was trying to ravish her. She felt, for the first time in a long time, safe, secure, wanted, protected. His tongue was so sweet and he was hungry with a passion she'd not seen since college.

He picked her up and she wrapped her legs around his back as he lowered her onto the floor. She was impressed with his strength. His body was so hard and muscular, like a finely chiseled work of art made by an ancient Greek sculptor. They kissed wildly, passionately, and then suddenly, gently, sensuously. He moved slowly downward caressing her body with his lips, massaging her with his tongue, until he reached her vagina. He had already told her on the phone about his sexual version of the ABC's and how no woman had ever made it to Z. Her response to him was that she could probably go through it three or four times and still not climax. At that, they began to view one another as a worthy challenge.

True enough, his tongue performed an alphabetical symphony on her clitoris. He literally traced every single letter. But before she could climax, and it was after several choruses, he got up, kissed her, smiled and said, "Not yet." When he placed his tongue in her mouth, she grabbed it and began to suck it the way she would suck his penis. From the way he reacted, she doubted if anyone had ever kissed him that way before. Then she began to guide him upward. He quickly caught the message. He placed his penis over her face and she gasped. It was so big and so long that she almost chickened out in fear!

She began to make love to his penis. It was so unique. In her hands it felt like silk and it was as smooth as melted chocolate in her mouth. She began to suck and lick and nibble his balls and he was like a puppy running frenzily to his new master. He could barely handle it. He snatched her up, carried her into his bedroom and closed the door. Despite the fact that she was extremely self-conscience about her out of shape body, he wanted the lights on. Later, he told her that he can tell when a woman climaxes; her pupils dilate. He wanted to see her pupils to make sure he knew she wasn't faking.

He began to suck and lick her vagina again. He actually made love to her and she to him in every position imaginable and then in some even she'd never heard of before. And the things he said! He'd pulled her on top of him and began to suck her very worn breasts. Being self-conscience, she said, "These breasts have nursed two babies," and she dropped her head.

His response was, "Let them nurse a third." At one point, he was on top of her and the upper portion of her body was hanging somewhat off the bed. He told her, as he stared deeply into her eyes, "I count it an honor and a pleasure being with you. It feels as if we are writing a verse to the oldest form of poetry known to man." She melted with each word, each stroke of his manliness, but he would not allow her to climax just yet.

He got up and she rolled him over. She poured the warm oils she'd brought on his back and massaged him. She couldn't help but admire how his long hours of working out everyday proved beneficial to his form. When she finished, he left the room. She could hear Boys to Men's video *I'll Make Love To You* playing in the other room. He'd had her to lie on her stomach, so she didn't know he had the whip cream until she felt it on her back. Her body trembled with expectation. His tongue felt so warm and so good.

His kisses were gentle, sweet. She felt lost in his touch and calming embrace.

As he turned her over to put whip cream on her vagina, he took his time eating and licking it off. He arose briefly to kiss her. He had whip cream on his lips and she licked it off. They enjoyed savoring the sweetness of one another's tongues.

When he finally inserted himself in her, she gasped with extreme pleasure. She almost came instantly. Sensing it, he stopped, smiled down at her and said, "Not yet." This he did four times and then said; "Now it is time to conquer you." He made her say his name and by the time he finally allowed her to climax, she felt as though she'd reached the highlight of a symphony composed by the most remarkable of artists.

When it was over, they both laid there in awe. He held her in his arms as her head rested across his chest. "Evette, you have to make a decision."

And she woke up, trembling and sweating…..

BEFORE

Another Attempt

A siren in the distance. She could faintly hear their voices. Everything sounded muffled, as if she was under water. She felt something on her face. It was an oxygen mask. The paramedics were rushing her into the emergency room. *I can't do anything right.* She thought, as she heard the doors fling open. *I'm tired of hurting! I don't want to be here! Why am I STILL here! You don't love me. You let all of this happen to me. Why can't you let me die?* Again, God gave no answer.

"What do we have here?" It was the doctor, she assumed. One of the paramedics handed him the bottle of Dylantin that she'd had taken and said, "It appears that she's taken over half the bottle. Her Sorority sisters found her unconscious in the dormitory. They said she'd been acting withdrawn all day and didn't feel like talking, which they say is totally not like her."

"Where'd she get the prescription pills from?" The doctor inquired.

"They belong to one of her sorority sisters." Said the paramedic.

"How can you be sure how much she's taken?"

"The girl told me she'd just had the prescription filled yesterday." The paramedics left the room.

"She's so young and beautiful." The nurse said. At that time, Evette was a nineteen-year-old sophomore at Jimmerson State University. She weighed only 98 lbs (fully clothed) but was solidly built and beautiful. She was lying there with her eyes closed; wishing she could experience a Calgon moment and be transported somewhere else. She finally opened her eyes.

"So, you don't value your life, huh, little girl?" It was the doctor. He was a middle-aged, white male. He was quite handsome. Evette was too ashamed to look him in the eye, so she turned her head. "Well, this will definitely be a day you will remember." He held up a black tube. "You see this? This is what I'm going to have to use to pump your stomach." Her eyes widened. "Open wide and take a deep breath. I'll put it down as swiftly as possible."

She did as he said and he pushed the tube down her throat. All she could do was cry as she felt this big black thing forcing its way inside of her. Instantly, she started vomiting. The sweet smell of pineapple juice began to fill the room.

"So, that's what you washed the pills down with, huh!" It was more of a statement than a question. "You young people never cease to amaze me. Things get hard. You think, 'I'll just kill myself.' That's your way of escaping isn't it? You forget about the people that you will be leaving behind; the people that love you; the people who have always been there for you. No, you can't see beyond the present circumstances. Can you?" He was shaking her stomach as he talked; making sure that everything down there came up.

When it was over, they took her into the intensive care unit, hooked a bunch of wires on her to monitor her heart. By now, her mother, aunt and a family friend had been informed and had driven to Rollins. Her mom had told the doctors that she'd had a history of heart murmurs as a child and that's why they had hooked her to the heart monitor. Evette could hear them outside. The doctor spoke to her sorors and frat brothers. "We're going to admit her to the top floor," the doctor said. Sorority sister, "But that's the mental ward. You can't do that! She's not crazy! She's just going through a lot of crap right now!" Her mother comes, "I want her to be released in my care." The doctor asks, "And who are you?" She responds, "I'm her mother. And I'm taking her home tonight."

Oh, God, I don't want her to see me like this. Just as Evette finished the thought, in she came. She looked broken.

"Baby, why?" She asked as tears began to stream down her cheeks. Evette wanted to talk to her, but the pain was so great until she couldn't open her mouth. All she could was drop her head, cry and say, "Mommie, I'm sorry. I didn't mean to hurt you."

"The doctors said that you can leave. We're taking you home."

She protested. "But I don't wanna go home. I want to stay here in Rollins with my Sorority sisters."

"Evette, if you stay here, they're going to admit you into Whitfield. Is that what you want? To be admitted into a mental institution? Get dressed. We're going to go get you something to eat."

The nurse came in. She took all of the wires off, took the IV out of her arm and took the oxygen mask off her face. She tried to stand up and almost fell. Her mother was there to hold her up. Their eyes met briefly and then, in shame, Evette turned away. Her mother smiled and said, "Don't worry. Momma's gotcha." She helped Evette get dressed and they went into the hall so that she could say goodbye to her friends. "Evette, we'll see you next semester, right?" One asked. "We'll see." She replied. They all embraced and then she left as she heard all of them wishing her well and telling her that they would be praying for her.

They stopped at Popeye's. Everyone tried to make conversation, but Evette ate in silence. If you obeyed the speed limits, it would take about three hours to get from Rollins to their hometown. They made it in about two hours. Her brother and sister were there but neither of them said anything. What can you say to your sister who has just tried, for the second time, to kill herself? Evette walked past them, went into their mother's bathroom and ran a hot bubble bath. She tried to wash away all of the pain, but some things just don't roll off like dirt, no matter how you scrub. She got dressed for bed and when she woke up the next day, it was around one o'clock in the afternoon. She felt as if they should have committed her. At least then she would have had someone to safely and privately talk to. Someone bound by law to keep her secrets.

It's something about a person who attempts suicide that most people don't understand. Never try to talk to them about it when it's still fresh. As soon as she got up and got dressed, all she heard was 'Evette, telephone.' All of the conversations went the same way.

"Evette, how are you doing? I heard about what happened. Are you all right?"

"Yes, I'm fine. Thanks for asking."

"So, why did you do it?"

"I don't wanna talk about it."

"Well, okay, maybe later. Bye."

"Goodbye."

The last time they told her the phone was for her it was her father. He'd left them and filed for divorce when she was age two and her sister was one. Since then, she'd only seen him about three times. Each time they'd talk with him, they had to tell him how old they were. She and her sister always felt hurt that he never seemed to care enough about them to even remember their birthdays.

"How ya doin' sweetheart?"

"I'm fine, daddy." She wanted to scream *how the hell do you think I'm doing? I just tried to kill myself for the second time! How do you think I'm doing?* "I'm doing fine."

"Sweetheart, I'm really sorry for not having been there for you guys all these years." She heard a crack in his voice.

"It's okay, daddy, really it is."

"Evette, why did you try to do it? Talk to me. You can take as long as you need to get it out. I'm listening, please open up to me."

And she did. There were so many things to tell him, but she told him about the thing that popped into her mind first. She told him about Uncle.

When they'd relocated from Chicago, it was quite a transition for her. She was twelve at the time and it wasn't easy to leave a city like Chicago and move to a small town. She was taken aback that there were people who still chopped cotton in the summer, willingly, for $20 a day! As they grew closer to Evette's father's side of the family she found Uncle to be the father she never had.

Her father silently listened as she told him one of her many secrets. He knew that Uncle was a prominent figure in the community and everyone seemed to love him, especially the children. It actually began when she was twelve and a half. Her sister, brother, cousins and she had gone to Uncle's workplace while they were out playing. He owned the vending machines there, so he opened one of them and gave them all an equal amount of quarters. Excitedly, Evette said, "I want all of the quarters" and he gave them to her. "Oh, thanks Uncle," She said and gave him a kiss. She was aiming for his cheek, but he turned his head and the kiss ended up on his lips. She withdrew and looked at him strangely and then shrugged it off as her imagination.

A couple of years later, when she was about fourteen, they were all asked to come to a 'family meeting' because one of their cousins had accused Uncle of trying to molest her. They lit into her like crazy. "You need to stop lying! You know Uncle would NEVER do anything like that to you or any other child!" Evette and her sister were asked if Uncle had ever tried to feel, fondle, or have sex with either of them and they said no. They were dismissed and eventually their cousin's parents separated because no one believed her accusation. Her father remembered the incident.

Well, that did it for the foundation. She told him about the night of her Junior Prom and how the date had gone bad. Evette had asked a homosexual to escort her to her prom. Sounds strange, but she knew he was gay when she asked him. What she didn't know, however, was that he went both ways. At the end of the date, he tried to make a pass at her. She reminded him who her Uncle was and when that didn't work, she told him that she would have one of her cousins from his hometown shoot him. Because everyone knew how crazy her cousin was, once he heard that, he took her back to her hometown. She knew her mother would beat her if she came home drunk, so she told her psycho date to drop her off at her Uncle's home.

It was around 11pm when he opened the door. He was fully dressed. She was crying as she told him about what had almost happened. He reminded her that she could not go home intoxicated and that she could sleep for a couple of hours and he would take her home. She rested on the couch and almost instantly fell asleep. She arose briefly into a state of semi consciousness and then drifted back. She had been awakened by gentle kisses, and what felt like a hand rubbing her breast.

Around 2am, Uncle woke her up and drove her home. She could vaguely remember what happened but she shrugged it off as a dream. Later that same year, it was discovered that Uncle had had an affair with a high school student. It was more than her precious aunt could bare and she filed for a divorce.

It was at this time, that Uncle hired her to be his maid. This was nothing new, because when he and her aunt were together, she would pay Evette to come clean up. She would come over every Wednesday to dust, wash clothes, sweep and mop. He would pay her $50 a week and that became her game money. She was a cheerleader and the money she made from housecleaning paid for her food on the road. Another perk, was that Uncle allowed her to have company that she was not able to have at home. The only thing he required was that she changes the sheets when she was done.

One evening, he came home a little early. Her lover had just left and she hadn't had time to change the bed.

"Evette, I don't mind you having company, but please change the sheets when you're done." He called from the bedroom.

"I'm sorry. He just left and I wasn't expecting you to be in so soon." She was embarrassed. She quickly began to strip the bed. She put the sheets in the washing machine and proceeded to put fresh linens on the bed. Uncle helped her. When they were finished, she turned to leave and he stopped her. He put both of his hands on her shoulders and held her in front of the mirror.

"You look so much like your aunt." She was frozen. "Did I ever tell you that every time I see you, I think of her?" She wanted to scream and run away, but she was frozen. He began to caress her shoulders. "I've wanted you since you were twelve years old." Her heart sank into the pit of her stomach and she wanted to throw up. "Remember when you came into the office that day and I gave all of you quarters from the machine? You tried to kiss me on the cheek but I purposefully turned my head. I wanted to know if your lips were as soft as they looked. You know what? They were."

She felt him as he began to slowly pull her backward toward the bed. She watched the whole thing through the mirror but it seemed as if it wasn't real. Like she was watching a movie. She looked at their reflections and saw him kiss her on the nape of her neck. She saw him caressing her breasts with his hands. She saw his tongue as he licked her ear. Evette watched in silent horror as he lowered her down upon the bed and promised her that he'd be gentle. When he lifted his leg to climb on top of her, she snapped. She began to hyperventilate and shake all over as she cried "Please don't do this to me! Please! Please don't!"

He jumped up immediately and began begging her not to tell her mother because she would kill him. He said that if that were to happen, she would be without a mother and a father. He then proceeded to give her things - a camera, a watch, a gold ring with opal stones that he never got a chance to give her aunt. Uncle promised her that he would leave town and begged that she tell no one about him.

She kept silent and he left town. There were those who had questioned as to whether something had happened between the two of them because of the drastic change in her behavior around him. Her father was very angry, but it was two years in the past. What could he do? He told her that he wanted her and her sister to spend the next summer with him.

She returned to school in the spring and tried to forget what had happened the previous semester. No one knew what had set her off and she didn't volunteer to tell. She couldn't tell them that what set it off was a man, yes, a man. He was a man that she loved more than life itself. Things had gone sour in their relationship, especially after she'd gone off to college. He never told her that he loved her and so she assumed that he didn't. She felt as though she was just good sex for him, and when she found out the truth about his feelings, it was too late. She offered to put her life on hold for him, but he rejected her.

After that, she stopped caring about herself. She began to drink almost every day. Sometimes, she would lie in her dorm room with a 40oz of beer in one hand and a cigarette in the other. She would smoke and drink until she passed out. As time passed, she added marijuana to the list. She was drowning and there was nothing that could be done about it. She still kept in touch with Love but not regularly. He was gone and she knew it. Afterwards, every man that came into her life served as a pale reminder him.

Spring semester flew by quickly. She was taking ROTC and had been asked to join the Army and go to Basics and A.I.T. during the summer because she'd out-shot everyone on the firing range. However, she didn't want to miss her first opportunity to visit her father. Things started out pretty well. Evette spent the first two weeks with him and his new wife and stepson. Later, she found herself at his ex-wife's home for the remainder of the summer. Her sister joined her around July. She'd spent the first half of the summer in Chicago with their mom's oldest sister.

While there, she met a young man named Weldon. He was from Philly and was spending the summer with his father for the first time as well. They instantly clicked and one week after meeting, they were sexually involved. He reacquainted her with the Quigi Board and introduced her to anal sex. By the time the summer ended, he'd taken her to Disney Land and had asked her to marry him. She couldn't believe she actually accepted his proposal. She didn't love him, but he was so sweet, she knew that eventually she would grow into it. Besides, the sex was GREAT and he reminded her so much of Love.

There was only one down side of the summer. The day her father took them to see Uncle. Evette died inside when her father made her give him a hug. It took a long time for her to forgive her father for doing that. She shared with him her pain, and he in turn ground salt into her wounds. Later, he told her he did it to see if Uncle showed any sort of reaction. If he had, her father would have shot him. However, that meant nothing to Evette. In her eyes, her father had betrayed her.

When she returned in the fall, she became a person that she didn't know. She began to wear spandex outfits, bra-like tops with mini skirts. She began to smoke and drink like never before. Evette was twenty years old, yet she felt like she'd lived all that there was to live. Her mind went back to her freshman year when she was pondering her life's situation. She remembered thinking *I have a job. I have good friends. I have money and clothes, but something is still missing.* Then it dawned on her. *God. God is what's missing in my life.* But since she didn't know where to find Him, she shrugged her shoulders and continued business as usual. There was emptiness within her and all the alcohol she consumed, all the joints she smoked, and all the sex she had, couldn't fill it.

Then one night, something strange happened. The professor of her Adolescent Psychology class let them leave after they finished their test. Usually, he'd make the students stay until he graded the papers. As she entered the glass doors to the dormitory, she noticed the weekly Bible Study was going on in the lobby.

An Unexpected Change

Hmm, Bible Study is still going on, Evette thought, as she made her way up stairs to find her girlfriends. She entered the room and asked her roommate Jessica where the others were. "They're out and won't be back any time soon. They thought you'd be in class until 9:30 and it's almost 8p.m." She asked what Evette's plans were, and she told her "same as usual - go out, get drunk and get laid. Not necessarily in that order." She winked and headed out the door.

In her mind, she wanted to go find her friends. She knew all of their hangouts so she figured it wouldn't take her long to catch up with them. Instead, she found herself grabbing their green pocket Bible. The thought crossed her mind that they only picked this Bible up when they were all high or drunk and alone with each other. That's when their pain and brokenness would really show. During those times, they would try to read and interpret the Bible as they cried because of their sad state of being. They all wanted to be better, and even though their actions said that they'd given up, their hearts still clung to the thought that one day things would be better. They would be better. Evette headed downstairs to Bible Study.

The man that taught was tall, dark, and handsome and wore a low cut afro. He was saying something about two different types of water baptism. She asked him what the difference was and he invited her to church. She told them "thanks, but no thanks." Then she found herself going to her room and changing clothes. She put on a pink and gray dress with pink pumps and freshened up her make-up. Next thing you know, she's in church.

She had no idea what the Bible Class was about because she kept falling asleep. She woke up one time and noticed that she was the only woman in the church that had on make-up. "Are you all right?" A woman sitting behind her asked. "I'm just noticing," Evette said, "that it seems like I'm the only woman in here with makeup on." "Oh, sweetie, don't mind that." When she woke up again, she found herself standing at the altar and a man was asking her if she wanted to be baptized. Evette agreed and they baptized her that night. The funny thing is that they had to dip her twice because not all of her went under water the first time. She thought to herself, *dag, I must really be messed up. They had to plunge me under water two times.* The first time she was baptized was when she was twelve years old. Her mother told her that if you come up choking that meant you were going to Hell. Wouldn't you know it, she came up choking! This time however, she didn't choke.

When they were leaving the church, it was as if a great burden had been lifted from her shoulders. She felt as if she was literally walking on air. She looked down at her feet to ensure that she was placing them carefully on each step. She actually felt as if she could fly away. She was told to come back the next night to 'tarry for the Holy Ghost.' She didn't understand what that meant, but if it felt anything like what she was feeling at that moment, she knew she wanted it.

Evette returned to the dorm with a glow on her face. Her girlfriends were there and they were upset. She told them where she'd been and they unloaded both barrels. They said that the church was an occult and they compared the pastor to Jim Jones. They demanded that she not go back. She asked them how they knew and if they'd ever been there. They hadn't, so that blew their little arguments as far as she was concerned.

Thursday couldn't come quick enough. As soon as her Marriage and the Family course let out, she was headed down the street to the church. She was met at the door by a middle aged woman and an older man. They took her into what they called a 'tarrying room' and told her to sit on the floor in front of one of the chairs. She thought it was rather strange, but she obeyed. There were other people in the room; college students, children, and men who'd been recently baptized and they were all sitting before chairs. The strange thing about it is that all the chairs had newspapers spread across them and toilet tissue was in the center.

The sister, Sharon, pulled out a Bible and turned to Acts chapter two, verse thirty-eight and guided her finger across the page as she read it aloud. She told Evette that she'd already been baptized and that what she was about to do now was receive the gift of the Holy Ghost. It sounded crazy, but Evette felt that if this was the way to God, then so be it. Sister Sharon asked her to get on her knees and hold onto the chair. She obeyed. She told her that she could say 'hallelujah', 'thank you, Jesus', or 'bless you, Jesus' as praise unto God. Evette chose 'thank you, Jesus.' She then demonstrated how she wanted Evette to say it and that was as loud and as fast as she possibly could. Evette did exactly as instructed.

Spit began to form in her mouth and when she tried to swallow, Sister Sharon told her to let it run on the tissue and the newspaper. *Oh, so that's what it's for*, she thought. Evette told her that was nasty and Sister Sharon said 'you've got to get rid of all your self-centered pride if you want Jesus'. She told Evette to take her mind off herself and picture Jesus hanging on the cross, bleeding and dying because of her sins. She also added that Evette should picture herself running to him and not to stop for anything. At the same time, she was to repent within herself for all of the wrong she'd done in life. *Man, after all the stuff I've done, I'm gonna be down here a long, long time,* she thought.

As fast as she could, she began to scream THANK YOU, JESUS! THANK YOU, JESUS! THANK YOU, JESUS! She pictured herself running to Him but she seemed so very far away. The closer she got, the more she cried. She began to talk to God in her mind. She begged Him to forgive her for all of the lies, the fornication, the suicide attempts, the drinking, and the drugs. She asked Him to forgive her for all of the people she'd hurt, for not forgiving the people who had hurt her, and the excessive partying. She could hear Sister Sharon's voice prompting and encouraging her all the way, like a mid-wife in a delivery room. Just then, she could see herself at the foot of the cross, and the blood of Jesus began to stream down. But right before it could reach her, she was snapped back into the reality of her environment.

"Calm down, little sister! Calm down!" She heard the older gentleman say. He was in his mid sixties and somewhat over weight. He wore glasses and had eyes that would melt your heart. He was a sweet old man. He was tarrying with a girl Evette remembered from campus. She had crashed a party they'd thrown and they were going to beat her up, but decided against it in the end.

"This is crazy! Show me in the Bible where it says we have to be down here like this! You people are crazy!" Carry said as she prepared to get up and leave.

They stopped her and showed her in Acts chapter two where the disciples 'tarried' in the Upper Room until they were filled with the Holy Ghost. They told everyone that they'd know when they received the Holy Ghost because they'd begin to speak in tongues, just like the apostles did on the day of Pentecost. At that, Carry quieted down and they proceeded to tell everyone what Evette would later label 'Tarry Room Horror Stories.'

There were two that stuck in Evette's mind. The first was about this lady who had come to the church and was baptized the same day. Her husband, a sinner, found out that she was at church 'tarrying for the Holy Ghost' and stormed into the room. He told her that she could either stay on her knees trying to 'get some damn Holy Ghost' or she could leave with him. She got up and left. One week later, she was dead. He came back to church, got baptized, received the Holy Ghost and later testified that he was sorry for being his wife's reason for going to Hell.

The second was of a woman, a backslider, whom a member had been inviting back to church for some time. Each time she was invited, she'd make up an excuse as to why she couldn't come. The last time, she was invited to a Friday night youth service and she turned it down saying that she would be there on Sunday morning. Later, that Friday night, she was home in bed and her boyfriend decided to play a prank on her. He straddled her chest while she was asleep and woke her up to a 357 Magnum pointed at her nose. He pulled the trigger, not knowing that there was one bullet in the chamber. She died instantly and never got a chance to return to God.

By the time they got finished talking, everyone was afraid to leave. They thought that God might allow something to happen to them and they would never get the opportunity to speak in tongues before they died. Needless to say, within days, every single one of them had experienced speaking in tongues.

That's when all hell broke loose. Evette's friends and associates thought she was just going through some religious faze, and gave her three months to snap out of it. After three months, they realized that she was very serious because she was still going to church every night. She was still reading her Bible at every opportunity she could find. She was still praying four times a day, and fasting (one meal a day) sometimes for five and six days a week.

The entire university campus was literally turned upside down. "Evette Williams is SAVED! I don't believe it." Others said, "If God can save Evette, I know He MUST be dealing with me." One by one, they came to the Lord. So much so until Evette was accused of trying to 'save the campus' but all she did was go to church and if someone asked her what caused her to change, she told them.

In January, the end of her three months, the very person she had intended on poisoning just months earlier, got saved. Evette had written a letter to one of her sex partners back then and had left it on the desk. Everyone read it but Jessica was the only one dumb enough to comment about it. Evette told her that she was going to poison her with embalming fluid. She was a cancer patient, so Evette didn't want to kill her; she just wanted to put enough drops in to put her in the hospital for a few days. She wanted to let her know that she was NOT the tree that she wanted to piss on or around, but God saved her before shc could do it. When Jessica saw the complete turn around Evette's life had taken, and how she was being consistent and genuine, she converted.

Gradually, Evette's best friends began to leave her alone. Not that she was pushing them away; they just no longer shared the same interests. Evette wanted to go to church. They wanted to continue partying. She wanted to read the Bible.

They wanted to get high. She wanted to spend her nights in prayer. They wanted to go get high and get laid. Their lifestyles automatically brought a wedge between them. She was finished with that life and she had no desire to return to it. She finally had peace and joy; things she'd always wanted but didn't know where to find. The void in her life had finally been filled and the former things no longer mattered. She was finally perfect. She was finally free.

Rude Awakenings

The night Jessica got baptized was something to remember. She came out of the pool speaking in tongues, but because she didn't acknowledge it for herself, no one said anything to her about it. They'd gotten a new roommate from Lansing, Michigan, named Tina. Tina and Evette stayed at the church as long as they could but then they got very tired and returned to the dorm. Around 1:30am everyone on the floor heard a scream in the hallway. Someone was screaming Evette's name. It was Jessica! Tina and Evette jumped up, looked at each other and smiled. They knew she had it! The three of them rejoiced until they couldn't rejoice any more. They watched Jessica as she fell asleep with a smile on her face. Two hours later, she woke up speaking in tongues. That's pretty much how the rest of the morning went.

About three days later, Evette was walking across campus, saw Reggie and her body began to want him. He was about six feet, seven inches tall, chocolate complexioned and pure muscle. He was the only man, at that time that ever caused her body to tremble with pleasure. He had a smile that would knock your socks off and there was a lot about him that reminded her of Love.

She stormed into the dorm room and slammed the door.

"You saw him didn't you?" Tina asked.

She looked sharply at Tina. "Yes!" She yelled and began to cry.

"And you wanted him, too, didn't you?" She continued.

"Yes." She was ashamed to admit it.

"Don't tell me you actually thought that being saved meant being inhuman?" She smiled.

"Tina, I'm saved now. Saints are not supposed to go through this. Saints are not supposed to have sexual desires."

She interrupted. "And who told you that? Where in Jesus' name did you get that from? How do you think saints get married? They have to have some sort of attraction."

"No one told me. I just figured that..."

"YOU just figured that, huh? Well, welcome to reality, sweetie. You've just learned your first lesson. Just because you're saved doesn't mean you're dead to your feelings and emotions. Surprise! You're still human."

Evette was totally disappointed. For some reason, she had assumed that being saved meant that she would never have sexual desires again. She spoke with another sister, who told her to fall on her face in prayer and ask God to make love to her. At first she thought she was crazy. She was thinking carnally. At any rate, she did what the sister said and told God that she wanted to be held, caressed, made love to, but didn't want to sin against Him. She asked Him to make love to her. After a while, she felt a peaceful presence in the room and by the time she finished speaking in tongues and worshipping God, all sexual desires were gone. He had satisfied her soul through praise, prayer and worship. She found herself desiring to get closer and closer to God like never before. She began to fast almost every day of the week, every week, to the point that she forgot about sex altogether.

Then, in the midst of serving God, she discovered that someone was interested in her. Gerald was sweetly saved, loved to pray, fasted regularly and attended all of the services. He was tall, of a slender build, about her complexion (cocoa beige) and had beautiful brown eyes and a boyish grin. After about two months, she realized that he'd been purposely sticking around after church so that he could give her a ride back to campus. At first, the car would be full but after a while she noticed that she was the only one. One night, he asked for her thoughts on relationships where the woman is a few years older than the man. She told him that she felt it was all right as long as they had a good understanding of each other. She told him that true love has no age limit and therefore it shouldn't matter. He smiled and then it dawned on her that he'd asked her a loaded question. She quickly got out of the car and said good night.

Several weeks later, he asked for her phone number and from then on they were inseparable. Evette was a junior in college and three years older than Gerald. He was a senior in high school and worked part-time at a fast food store, but they had connected. Probably a bit too well. They began to get common with each other. They would casually hold hands, listen to love songs, and sit romantically in each other's presence at his home. His mother loved Evette and she was crazy about her as well. Eventually, they picked out wedding rings and began to talk about how good it would be to be married to each other.

One night they went to Pizza Hut for dinner. When they arrived at the church, they decided to spend time with each other instead of going to choir rehearsal. That was their first big mistake. They returned to his home and when his parents went to bed, they sat up watching Black Entertainment Television's Midnight Love segment. He noticed that her back was aching and offered to rub her shoulders. That was their second big mistake, because she felt as if something had come alive within her, something that was supposed to remain dead. She wanted to be held by him, to kiss him, to rest her head on his shoulder. They went into his bedroom. He lay on top of her and they slowly and gently kissed.

Then it happened. He pulled her skirt up and began fingering her vagina. She got scared. All she wanted was to be held, kissed, and comforted. She didn't want to have sex and worst of all; neither of them was protected against pregnancy. She began to cry and ask him to get up, but he pushed her panties to the side and entered her anyway. He didn't stop until he'd climaxed and then he withdrew. Evette laid there crying in a fetal position. Then it dawned on him and he asked her to forgive him for raping her. He allowed her to get herself together and then he took her back to the campus. The entire way back, they both cried as he kept asking her to forgive him. She told him she would. They then considered the possibility of her being pregnant and how he was only eighteen and neither of them was ready for that type of responsibility.

When she came into the dorm room, she immediately climbed up to her bed on the top bunk. She laid there in a fetal position and cried for hours. Tina knew instantly that something had occurred but Evette neither confirmed nor denied her allegations. She just laid there and cried. Besides, by that time she had lost a lot of respect for Tina. One evening when she came in from her last class of the day, she asked Evette a question that disturbed her.

"Evette, if you woke up in the middle of the night and discovered that someone was performing oral sex on you what would you do?" She asked. The devil knew that oral sex was a great weakness of hers.

"I don't know." She replied.

"What if you were right on the brink of orgasm and you looked down and saw that it was a woman? Would you make her stop or would you let her climax you?"

"Girl! Are you crazy! That's nasty! I would make her stop!" She yelled.

"If you were about to cum, you would make her stop?" She continued.

"Yes!"

"Why?" She just kept prying.

"Because it's nasty, it's wrong, and I believe that if you are going to sin, you should sin right. Homosexuality and lesbianism is abnormal and that's why God destroyed Sodom and Gomorrah." After that, she left Evette alone and targeted Jessica who wasn't as strong.

Tina quickly spread the rumor around church that Gerald and Evette had committed fornication. One Sunday morning, one of the Bishop's daughter's came to her and told her to throw herself on the mercy of her father, but when she and Gerald went to confess, he said Evette seduced him. She couldn't say a word. She sat in silence as the Bishop accused her of doing 'to him what Eve did to Adam' and sentenced her to return to the altar and re-tarry for the Holy Ghost. He said that it was because of Gerald's honesty that he wasn't going to disfellowship them. Evette returned to the altar as she was told to do. Shortly afterwards, she learned that the entire time Gerald was seeing her, he was also seeing one of the Bishop's nieces behind her back. She was beyond hurt.

One Monday night, she called him on his job and told him she felt that she needed to spend more time trying to get closer to the Lord. He knew she was breaking up with him and he asked her to pray for him when she went to church that night. She did. Their breakup affected her more than she thought it would. It became difficult for her to come to church and see him with his new interest, especially when Evette saw that he was treating her far better than when they were together. What made matters worse, one of her roommates told her that Cynthia was built better than her, had longer, prettier hair, could sing, dressed better, was of a brighter complexion and was in the Bishop's family. She told Evette that she was an untalented nobody, with no great church family name attached to her and therefore no man would want her. She had nothing to offer.

Evette cried herself to sleep every night for a week. Then one night, one of the mothers of the church had a talk with her. Thank God for genuine church mothers. She reminded Evette of how beautiful, gifted and intelligent she was. Then she taught her something that she would never forget; she taught her how to worship God. She taught her to thank God for every tear, every pain, and every trial. She taught her how to get in the face of God and not let Him go. Evette knew God as her savior and now she was learning that He is also her friend.

After her experience with her first boyfriend in the church, she began going out with other brothers. She'd been proposed to a couple of times, but a blind person could see that those guys just wanted to get married so that they could have sex without condemnation. Though she wanted to be married, she refused to be used like that. She wanted sex just like the next person, but she didn't want that to be the driving force behind entering into a 'til death do you part' situation.

By this time, she'd been struggling with masturbation for two years. Though she felt guilty and condemned about it, she found it difficult to stop. She justified her behavior by telling herself that masturbating was better than fornicating and that 'the Lord knows my heart.' She told herself that it was the 'lesser of two evils,' but in her heart she knew she was wrong. If Jesus said that a man looking upon a woman and lusting after her was the same as committing adultery, surely what she was doing was no different. In her mind, she relived all of her 'best sex' experiences with various men. Her pastor told her that she needed to get married - though he didn't think she was ready at the time. She was only twenty-two years old and no matter what, if she got married, she wanted it to be for love, not sex.

Then something heart stopping happened. She'd just returned from a lingerie shower and one of her roommates told her that she'd had a phone call. She thought nothing of it, until she was told that it was Love and that he said he would call her back at 11pm. She looked at the clock and saw that it was almost that time. She lost her breath, her heart stopped, and she began to literally tremble. The phone rang and she just stood there looking at it. It must have rung about four times before she finally picked it up.

It was Love. He asked how she was doing and it was all Evette could do to muster up the strength to sweetly say "fine." They talked for hours about everything and she realized that she was still very much in love with him. Around 4:30am, he asked if she wanted to come home for the July 4th weekend and she said yes. It was 5am when they hung up and he told her he was on his way. As best as she could, she gave him directions to the house. Despite the heat, she asked him not to wear shorts. She was extremely sleepy but flew through the house packing as carefully but as swiftly as possible. She took a scented bath, put on her best perfume, got dressed and waited anxiously.

Around 7am she heard a soft knock on the door. Her heart jumped. She thought, *man he must have left as soon as we hung up the phone.* She waited until he knocked again and then she asked who it was. He said his name and she opened the door. She couldn't believe how good he looked. He smiled and she melted. He was actually standing there in a white, short-sleeved, cotton shirt and you guessed it, shorts! They were khaki and fit perfectly. She didn't look long, because she noticed that her body began to respond. Being the southern gentleman that he was, he took her bags and put them in the trunk of his car. His baby sister was with him and she got in the back seat when she saw them come out of the house. They went to Popeye's for breakfast and conversation and then they were off.

Instead of taking her home, he took her to his mom's house. It was around 10am when they arrived and they all bathed again and changed clothes. Love and Evette slept in his old bedroom, in separate beds, though. It was one of the most challenging moments she'd experienced in a long time; to be behind closed doors, alone and in bed while the one man she loved more than herself laid less than ten feet away from her and they were not touching each other!

They slept through lunch and after they woke up, Evette and his mom began to prepare dinner. This was the first time that she and Evette actually got along. Love smiled every time he came through the kitchen and saw them laughing and talking. She could see that Evette was no longer the same person that she was when Love first started seeing each her four years earlier and they had a good time talking about God and various things in the Bible.

Before they knew it, it was dark, Evette had made a pass at him and he reminded her that real men prefer to make the first moves and that aggressiveness in a woman is a turn-off. Thus, she was rebuked. It was almost 10pm when they arrived at Evette's mother's home. They were glad to see her. Later, her mom told her that Love had driven around town until he found someone that knew where they'd moved to and then he got the number from them. In other words, he was searching for Evette, which she thought was very romantic of him.

She spent July 4th with Love and his family and they had a wonderful time. Later, that night, they drove out to their 'spot' and talked. It was a beautiful, star-filled night. It was almost as if you could just reach up and grab a handful of stars. You could hear the crickets in the background and see the town lights off in the distance across the field. He held her hand, they looked into each other's eyes, and she melted like butter on a hot, wooden stove. In her mind, she wondered if he could see how very much she loved him. They began to gently caress each other as they embraced. His lips were so soft and luscious and he remembered her body like a well-read book.

He mounted her like a warrior victoriously returning home from battle and she wrapped her legs around his waist. Every fiber of her being wanted him, to have him, to hold him, to be made love to by him, to be his and his alone. Then she felt him against her and reality set in.

"No, Love, I can't." She whispered. He kept kissing the one spot that always brought her literally to her knees. She continued. "I haven't had sex in two years. I'm not on any birth control. What if I get pregnant?"

"I want you to have my baby." He said. "I want you to get pregnant."

Everything within her dissolved when she heard him say that because she *wanted* to have his child. She *wanted* to have a tangible combination of the two of them to commemorate the love they shared. He sweetly whispered in her ear that he loved her as he continued hitting every major spot on her body. He wanted her to verbally say 'yes.' And Evette wanted to say 'yes.' In fact, every part of her body was screaming 'Yes! Yes! Heck yes!' She quivered at every touch, melted with each kiss. Finally, when she opened her mouth to respond, she yelled.

"Oh, God! Save me, Jesus! Lord, I'm so sorry! Please forgive me, God! I'm so sorry!" And she started to cry. In hearing that, all of a sudden he felt as if he was Satan personified. He released her from his embrace and shamefully got up and sat in his seat with his head in his hands.

After that night, they continued to spend every waking moment together. As always, when he came to her mom's home and sat in the chair, Evette sat at his feet with her head resting on his lap. He was the only man that she'd ever done that to. He took her back to Rollins and from that day forward, they talked every day on the phone. She prayed every night for him to convert to her religion.

In the midst of all of this, the President had sent troops to Kuwait for what he called 'Desert Shield.' Since Saddam Hussein was not showing any signs whatsoever of cooperating, 'Desert Shield' turned into 'Desert Storm' and the men and women of the US military were in battle.

Everyone Evette knew who'd joined the military was in the Middle East and they prayed daily as never before. There were threats of chemical and germ warfare and Israel was being continuously bombed with SCUD missiles. Everyone was afraid that one hint of retaliation on Israel's part would cause all of the US' Muslim allies to turn, but Israel proved her strength and restrained from fighting back.

By the time the ground war was initiated, Evette's brother, Eugene, was on the front lines. They paved the way for the rest of the soldiers. They must have been frightened beyond words because they were just babies. Her brother had never killed anything bigger than a mouse and now here he was barely legal (21) and making the ultimate choice that any young man can make - to fight for his country. Evette was relieved when it was over and she'd received a letter from him. Even though he cursed her out for not writing him while he was there (she didn't know what to say), she was just glad that he was home. He was fine, physically anyway, because only God can heal the mental scars of war. One would venture to say that the US had won Desert Storm. Though Saddam Hussein still remained in power, they did evacuate Kuwait (after setting several oil fields on fire). He was an enemy that the USA had created, but the President spanked him very well and put him back in his place if only for the moment.

Just when Evette thought that everything was going well, Love called her and told her that he wanted to remain Baptist. She was crushed. It would be eleven years before she would see or hear from him again.

***

The following year, for whatever reason, Bishop decided that he and the choir should travel. They'd been invited to Michigan. Bishop was the guest speaker for a youth conference and they were the guest choir. The trip up there went pretty well. Everyone had fun, despite the fact that they'd been put on voice rest and couldn't speak louder than a whisper, if at all.

Bishop had paid for a room for those who didn't have any money for the trip and the minister of music ensured that Evette was the one given the key. She was put in charge of who she wanted to be in the room with her.

The group she was with had fun driving around and getting lost. The women felt that it was a shame that even when a woman is holding a map, a man STILL won't take directions from her. That morning, on the way back to the hotel, she found herself with a different group of young people. They all got along well and had lots of laughs together. There was one particular person that Evette instantly clicked with because he reminded her of Love. Every time you turned around, they were all together but in the midst of the group, Jamal and Evette began to bond.

Jamal was about five feet and eleven inches tall, high yellow (as they say down south), of a slender build and had the cutest smile. He loved God with a passion. He was a pre-med. student at Tugaloo College at the time and was about four years younger than her. To talk to him, you'd never guess how young he was. He began to flirt with her by complementing her every time she turned around. "Oh, Sister Evette, I love the way you worship the Lord." "Sister Evette, you look very sanctified in that dress." "A man sure would be blessed to have you by his side." She found herself flattered.

Jamal was such a charming man and could actually hold a decent conversation on various topics. Evette appreciated the fact that they could debate certain issues and still laugh with each other when they were done. Neither of them took offense and that, to her, was a good thing.

Their last leg on the trip was to Lansing, Michigan where Bishop was asked to preach for a Sunday morning service. Of course, the choir backed him up. Later, they all changed in the church's rest rooms and then they were headed back to Mississippi. She was extremely tired because they'd all stayed up the night before laughing and driving around for food. She sat at the back of the bus in the same seat she'd sat in on the way up. This time, however, Jamal came and sat beside her. When she became sleepy, he put a pillow on his lap and told her to rest her head on it. She did. She couldn't believe how warm and safe she felt, nothing sensual, just peaceful.

He began to stroke her hair and then he felt her body tense up. He assured her that he was not trying to make a pass at her. He told her that a few years earlier, he'd had a cat that liked to rest on his lap and be stroked to sleep. She relaxed and before long, she was asleep.

When they made it back to Rollins, Jamal and Evette were like shadows. He would come over whenever she would have a dinner party and he always complemented her cooking. They never sat in church together and that was fine. They both wanted to concentrate on the word of God, not each other. They were becoming good friends. Before long, he began to stop by her job to pick her up and take her home. On occasions, he would pop up unannounced at her home to take her out to lunch or dinner. She found herself rearranging her plans to accommodate him.

One day, as they were hanging out in the mall, they passed by a jewelry store. He wanted to go in and so they did. He watched, as she seemed to pick the most expensive pieces of jewelry in each set. She couldn't help it if she had naturally expensive taste. He smiled as he watched her face light up at even the simplest things. Later that afternoon, he asked her to describe her dream home to him.

"My dream home will be beautiful, yet simple. I want a huge front and back yard so that my children will have lots of room to play. I want the house to have four or five bedrooms and be two stories high. I want a balcony up top and a deck out back. I want it to be enclosed with a white picket fence and I want a nice, big drive way around the side so that my guests won't have to worry about parking." He drove around until he found the home that he said fit that description and it was gorgeous. He assured her that one day she would have it.

Two weeks later, they were driving around listening to this new Gospel artist named John P. Kee when he noticed her writing a list.

"What's that you're writing?" He asked.

"Oh, just a list." She said.

"I can see that. What kind of list is it? Do you need to go to the grocery store or something?"

"No. Actually, it's a list of all of the qualifications I want in my husband." She replied with a smile.

They stopped for the red light. He stared deep into her eyes and asked, "I didn't know you were seeing someone."

She laughed. "I'm not, silly. It's a faith list. I'm writing down everything I want God to bless him to be whenever He decides to give me to someone."

"Give you to someone? What do you mean by that?"

"Well, the Bible says that 'whosoever finds a wife finds a good thing and obtains the favor of the Lord.' So, when God blesses him to 'find' me, I want him to possess all of these qualities."

He asked again, "But what do you mean by 'give you to someone?'"

"Just like in the garden. God gave Eve to Adam. Remember?" She said.

"Yeah, but when Adam blamed God for giving him Eve after he'd eaten the forbidden fruit, God no longer played match maker. You just quoted the scripture that proves it. 'Who ever finds his own wife obtains God's favor.'"

"I see someone's been studying." She said. "But whatever the case may be, these are the qualities that I want him to posses."

"Do you mind sharing some of them with me?" He asked.

"No, I don't mind at all. Number one, he MUST be saved."

"I'm saved." He said.

"Number two, he must pay tithes and offerings."

"I do that and faithfully I might add." He said, holding up one finger to drive his point home. "What else."

"Number three, he must know the word of God."

He slightly dropped his head and said, "I'm still working on that one. Continue."

"Number four, he must be family oriented."

"I love kids." At this point, Evette began to catch on but she didn't want to accept it. He was her friend and that's how she saw him.

"Number five; I want him to be able to play the drums." She giggled.

"The drums? Why the drums?"

"Because I like the way they sound. What's a song without drums?"

"You can be strange at times Evette Williams, very strange indeed." He said as he shook his head.

"Never you mind. My husband will love it." She replied. He looked at her and said, "I'm sure he will." Then he turned his eyes back to the road. "I'm sure he'll love every detail about you."

She cleared her throat. "So, Jamal, what is it that you want in a wife? Don't tell me, she has to be fine. She has to have a degree. She has to be able to sing. She has to be three years younger than you." He interrupted.

"Are you saying that I'm vain and shallow?" He was slightly offended. She'd never seen him like that before.

"I was just joking, Jamal. Come on."

"Actually, she has to be like you. Preferably, you." She was stunned. "Are you surprised? You are, aren't you?"

"I didn't think I was your type." Evette said.

"And what did I do to make you think that?" He asked.

"Well, for one thing, Jamal, I'm four years older than you. I'm too old."

"Evette, the moment we held our first conversation in Detroit, I knew you were the one for me. You have a great personality. You're easy to talk to and you can hold intelligent conversations. You're funny and easy to get along with. You have depth Evette and you're real. Also, you're an excellent cook and a wonderful friend."

"But I'm too old for you, Jamal."

"You can't tell me that you don't care for me, Evette." He demanded more than stated.

"I do care about you as a friend and nothing more. Because of our age difference, I've never considered the possibility of us getting together."

"Evette, would it surprise you to know that the last woman I dated before I got saved was ten years older than me? She was the cat that liked to be stroked to sleep. You're actually the youngest woman I've ever been truly interested in."

"What!" She was shocked. "I still can't court you." She said.

"Why?" He demanded.

"Heavens, man! I'm too young." They both burst into laughter. He pulled into her driveway and she hopped out. Turning around abruptly, she said, "I once loved someone who was younger than me and I still do love him."

"What happened?" He asked a question that he already knew the answer to.

"By the time I came to my senses, it was too late. I offered to wait for him, but he rejected me. I really don't want to be hurt again, Jamal, and you remind me too much of him."

"But I'm not him, Evette. I love you and I would never hurt you."

"Don't make promises you can't keep." She walked away and went straight into the house without looking back. That night, she heard a strange sound coming from the music area. It was Jamal and he was on the drums trying his best to keep up with the organ and the keyboards. He saw her looking and saluted her with one of the sticks. She had to laugh out loud.

For the next six months he became like a steady stream of water that runs gently across a hard rock. He began to wear her down. She found herself anticipating his calls, looking around church for him after services and taking advantage of every opportunity for him to walk her home. She was a member of the waiters and waitresses committee, so he joined too. She was a member of the choir, so he joined too. She volunteered to clean the church on her days off work and he did too. She was falling for him. Slowly, wonderfully, falling for him and then just as mysteriously as it began, it ended.

Jamal stopped calling her. He stopped picking her up from work. He stopped walking her home after services. He even stopped speaking to her. Later, she found out that a brother, who was interested in her and whom she had given the cold shoulder to, had told him about Gerald. She was mortified that he didn't come to her and talk to her about it, but instead believed what someone else told him. The rumor was that she had seduced Gerald but he and Evette knew what actually happened.

Evette then threw herself into working around the church like never before. She pushed men and marriage out of her mind and focused on the things of the Lord.

At First Sight

The national convention for the organization was fast approaching. Evette requested to have that entire week off from work so that she could serve in the kitchen, clean up, and to sing with the choir.

When July arrived, most of the waitresses were backing out of serving because they claimed that they wanted to 'meet their husbands and that couldn't be done while serving in the kitchen.' Evette told one sister, "Are you kidding? Serving is the best place to meet your husband. After all, if he sees you dressed up during service, you're just another well-dressed sister that he will soon forget. But, if he sees you every day, three and four times a day serving in the dining hall, he'll be more likely to remember you." That argument actually worked! She really could have cared less about meeting someone. She just didn't want everyone backing out because that would mean more work for all the others.

That Thursday, she came to the church early so that she could fill all of the salt, pepper, and sugar dispensers. It was a menial task that no one really wanted to do, but Evette realized that even small things become big issues when left undone. She was wearing hard bottomed work shoes, a pleated denim skirt that came to her ankles, no stockings, a red cheerleader T-shirt from high school and her hair was loose but half curled. In short, she was looking like Cinderella before the change.

"Sister Evette, you'd better hurry if you plan on being in the mass choir. Rehearsal is about to start." One of the brothers yelled through the dining hall door. She quickly finished filling up the last sugar dispenser, wiped the table and put everything away. The church cooks had started cutting up chickens around 7am and she carried the smell of it. She washed her hands and headed to the annex sanctuary.

The choir directors had the altos on the left side of the sanctuary and the sopranos on the right. The tenors were to sit in the choir stand. She felt so out of place. Everyone there was dressed to kill and there she was looking and feeling like a chitterling in the midst of a bah-mitzvah. The casual clothes that these ladies wore looked like something she'd wear on a Sunday morning.

As she sunk in her seat, the side entrance to the choir stand opened and this fine, mocha skinned brother walked in. He had the most beautiful eyes you'd ever want to see and he was very well dressed. Behind him, there came a brown skinned brother who was casually dressed. He was cute, too, and wore a big, welcoming smile. At that moment, their eyes met.

They kept making eye contact throughout the rehearsal. It was almost childish. During the mid-day break for lunch, she ran home (across the parking lot) took a bath, changed clothes, bumped a few curls in her hair, sprayed on some Victoria's Secret perfume and came back to finish eating. She laughed within herself when she saw his eyes buck as she walked into the dining area. She smiled at him and sat down on the opposite side of the room to eat.

Later that evening, he approached her with another young man. He stood there smiling while the other guy asked all the questions.

"Praise the Lord." He said.

"Praise the Lord." Evette replied.

"Are you a member of this church?" He asked.

"Did the waitress uniform give me away?" They both laughed.

"She's got a sense of humor." The guy said.

"What's your name?" He asked.

"Evette Williams."

"His name is Alexander Worthington." The young man said as he pointed to Alexander.

"What's the matter with him?" She said as she pointed to Alexander. "He can't speak for himself?"

"Actually, I can." Alexander said as he extended his hand to shake hers. She put her hands on her hips.

"Don't you know that it is improper for a gentleman to extend his hand to shake a lady's hand? The lady is to extend her hand first." She busted on him.

"You're right. I didn't mean to offend you." He said.

She smiled. "I'm not offended, and I'm still not going to shake your hand. I have to go serve. They're pretty strict about things like that. Are you dining with us today?"

"Yeah, I think I will."

"How old are you?" The other guy asked.

"Man, you're not supposed to ask a woman a question like that." She looked him up and down and then turned to Alexander and asked, "Where'd you get him from? Why don't you ask your own questions?"

"How old are you, Sister Evette?" Alexander asked.

"How old do I look? And be careful when you answer." She raised a threatening eyebrow as she smiled.

"You look like you're about nineteen." Alexander said.

"I'm not. I'm twenty-three. How old are you?"

"How old do I look to you?" Alexander asked.

"You look like you're about twenty-one, maybe twenty-two."

"Man, she hit it right on the nose." The other guy was starting to get on her nerves.

"I'll be twenty-two in December." Alexander said. Someone called out Alexander's name. It was another brother and they both looked back to see who it was. By the time they turned back around, Evette was gone.

Half an hour later, when the doors were opened for dinner, she saw Alexander come in. After that, every time the doors were unlocked, he was there. Sometimes, he would be sitting there sipping hot tea and watching her with a smile.

"There he is again, girl." One waitress said to her.

"Who?" She asked as she stepped to the door.

"Your admirer."

"Oh, my God. It is him." She peeked out of the door.

"Ooow! Evette, girl, he's fine."

"Can we get started setting up for dinner now?" She asked.

When the doors swung open for the dinner crowd, they were all strategically placed in the dining all and began to sing 'Come and dine.' Evette was stationed to at the senior's area but Alexander kept calling her to serve him things.

"Excuse me, Sister Evette, but would you please give me some more tea?"

"Yes, brother Worthington?" She was surprised that she even remembered his name. She made it a point of remaining very formal with him.

"Excuse me, Sister Evette, but they would like to have more macaroni and cheese." He pointed to a group of people seated at the table with him.

"Excuse me, Sister Evette."

"Yes, brother Worthington?" He was starting to get on her nerves, but she smiled anyway because she knew that it was just a test. Later, she found out that the group he'd had her to serve was actually his family and he was trying to give them an impression of her. She was glad that she maintained her composure.

As the days passed, all she wanted to do was work. She was at the church from 7pm until 2am the next morning. She pushed herself as hard as she could until she almost collapsed in the dining hall one evening. She was wiping down a table and when she got ready to pick up the tray a sharp pain went through her chest.

"Evette, are you all right?" She heard one of the deacons ask. At that moment, Bishop and other pastors and their wives put their hands on her and began to pray. Bishop told her that he didn't want to see her in the kitchen until the Bishop's banquet on Friday night.

That night, Alexander seemed excited that she wasn't working in the kitchen. He was sorry that she'd gotten sick, but this meant that they finally had a chance to sit down and talk. Evette found him to be quite refreshing. Of course, he reminded her of Love. He had the same hair texture, was of a quiet demeanor, and a perfect gentleman. She admired the fact that he never tried to flirt with her and he didn't approach her with any tired, played-out church lines. There is nothing, absolutely nothing worse than a church pick-up line! She also admired this innocent manner in which he carried himself.

After about thirty minutes, he cut to the chase.

"Sister Evette, do you believe that long distance relationships can work?" He asked.

"Well." She hesitated. "I believe that if it's God's will for the two to be together then it can work. I think both people have to know what they want and know that what they want is found in each other. Then and only then, can it really work".

He smiled.

"You know what I've always heard?" He asked.

"What's that?"

"I've always heard that you can tell when God puts two people together because they always look alike."

"I've heard that, too." She added. "As a matter of fact, when I first got saved, there were several couples in church that I thought were brother and sister, but they were actually husband and wife. So, I'd have to agree with you."

They got up, began to walk toward the lobby area and were approached by a man who appeared to be in his mid-forties. He looked excited as he approached, so she assumed that he knew Alexander.

"Brother Worthington, Praise the Lord." They shook hands and then the gentleman looked at her and said to Alexander, "Aren't you going to introduce me to your sister?"

They looked at each other with their mouths slightly opened. "Well, this isn't my sister. We just met this week. This is sister Evette Williams."

He shook her hand. "Please to meet you, Sister Williams." He pointed at Alexander and smiled. "This is a nice brother, a very fine brother, indeed. Any woman would be blessed to have him." He patted Alexander on the shoulder, smiled again at Evette and began to walk off. "A very fine brother, indeed. Remember that." He was gone. Later, Alexander told her that he was an Elder in one of their Sister Churches on the east coast and had known Alexander since he was a little boy.

Alexander and Evette seemed to get along very well and before she knew it, he'd asked her out to dinner. They went to Shoney's and the conversation flowed from one subject to another. Afterwards, they went to the mall and she picked out a tie for him. Maybe a woman just wouldn't be a woman if she didn't try to pull at least one trick, so when they passed by one of the department stores, she asked him to fill out the application for the credit card. They offered you a free gift, just for filling it out. While he was writing, she veered over his shoulder to see what he put in the section marked 'income' to see how much money he made. It wasn't much.

They returned to church and when service began, she put him to her ultimate test. She sat beside him during the service. She wanted to see if he would still praise God with her sitting beside him and he did! So, there they stood, praising God together. The reason it meant so much to her is because she'd seen so many women in church who were vibrant and active until they got married. Marriage seemed to drain all the life out of them. She'd promised herself that when she got married, she would not allow that to happen to her.

After service, they went into the fellowship hall where Alexander introduced her to his pastor. The fellowship hall could hold six hundred people and, like everything else, it was beautifully decorated. Bishop taught that God's house deserved the very best and everyone saw to that it did. The church was so immaculate. Someone had made videotapes of the entire building and they were selling them for $20 each. They told people they could 'take the temple home' with them.

"Alexander, would you please buy a sprite for me from the machine?" She asked.

"Sure." He replied. "I'll be right back." Evette turned to his pastor.

"Pastor, I wanted to ask you a question about Brother Worthington."

"Sure daughter. You can ask me anything you want about him." He stated.

"I want to know whether or not Brother Worthington pays his tithes and offerings faithfully to the church."

"Oh, yes. He is very faithful to the ministry." At that moment, Alexander walked up.

"Thank you, Pastor." Alexander could tell that they'd just finished talking about him.

By the time the convention ended, they felt as if they'd known each other for years. He told her that she was the first woman he'd ever taken out on a date and she felt extremely honored. She could tell that he was a virgin and she was quite impressed by that. It showed that he was totally committed to God and being an example of holiness - she only wished she could have had the same testimony.

"I don't want you to think that I'm being forward, but Sister Evette, may I have your address and phone number, please?" He shyly asked and she gave it to him on the smallest piece of paper she could find. "Aren't you going to ask for my address?"

"No." She smiled. "I'll get it off your first letter." They hugged each other and said goodbye. One week later, she received a letter from him.

"Evette!" One of her roommates shouted into the back room. There were five of them who lived in a three-bedroom house that was owned by the church. Naturally and spiritually, Evette was the 'baby' and was thus treated as such.

"What is it Tammy?" Evette yelled back.

"You have a letter from Baltimore, Maryland." She came into the room smiling. "It's from the brother that you met last week during the convention."

"I don't believe it."

"Believe it, girl, 'cause here it is." She handed her the letter.

"Oh, my God." He'd actually written. She sat on the couch and must have read his letter at least ten times before she stuck it in her Bible and headed to church. She was so excited. She showed the letter to everyone that she was acquainted with. It was so beautiful and spiritual and innocent. From that point on, they wrote each other every week. Then one day, she received a letter from him stating that he and his pastor would be visiting her for Thanksgiving weekend. She was elated!

By this time, she had moved out of the house with the other four women and had moved into one of the apartments that the church owned. She had a new roommate whose mother had put her out of the house because she wanted to be saved.

She was quit a pistol but nevertheless at times she could be as sweet as could be. She was about eighteen years old and expecting her first child. Evette was like the 'big sister' she never had. Not that she had a little sister just that she was the only girl. They were both excited and must have spent about three weeks getting Evette's wardrobe ready.

Well, they finally showed up on Friday evening. Since Evette had moved and he didn't know exactly where, he and his pastor came to the church after they'd checked into their hotel. They had a wonderful time in service together. She was the envy of quite a few women because this handsome, saved man came all the way from the East Coast just to spend time in her presence.

That Saturday, Alexander and his pastor came over to her apartment and met her roommate. After she left with her mother, the pastor left to rest at the hotel. Evette had found out what Alexander's favorite meal was and had prepared it. He loved spinach, macaroni and cheese, candied yams, fried chicken, and cornbread. Also, for dessert, she fixed lemon pie. They washed it down with iced tea. By the time he finished eating, he looked deep into her eyes and said, "Evette, would you be mine?" Of course, she agreed and thus their relationship began.

Within the time that they courted the telephone company must have made a fortune because they were daily on the phone with each other. She'd call him collect, of course. She must have written him at least three to four letters a week, gradually pouring her heart and soul out to him, but his letters seemed to maintain a very formal tone.

In March of 1992, Alexander purchased a round trip plane ticket to Baltimore for Evette. She arrived that Wednesday morning and was picked up at the Baltimore Washington International airport by the pastor. They went to breakfast at McDonald's where they spent about an hour conversing. He talked to her about the background of Maryland and she was impressed that such a small state could contain so much history. Instead of taking her straight to the home where she'd be staying, he drove around for a while showing her various sites.

They drove past The Washington Monument, the Inner Harbor, the Trade Center, Johns Hopkins, the Baltimore Museum of Art, and The College of Notre Dame, to name a few. They went to the pastor's home where she was introduced to his wife and told that there had been a change of plans. She would not be staying with them after all because the person who was working on their home had not finished the renovations in time for her arrival. She was taken to one of the aunt's homes where she put her things away.

Finally, they arrived at Alexander's house. By now, it was early evening. His mother, oldest sister, her children and several of his brothers greeted her at the door. Alexander had not arrived home from work yet, which gave his mom and Evette a chance to do some things. She found them all to be quite friendly and entertaining as they treated her like one of the family. She was extremely tired, though, because she had not slept for two days. At that time, she worked as a certified nurse's assistant at one of the nursing homes at Whitfield.

His great aunt showed up and then they were headed on a shopping spree. They must have gone to about four different malls. Evette dozed off in the van several times. When they made it back, Alexander was there and he greeted her at the door with a big hug. That night, his mom made a wonderful dinner and everyone sat at the table together laughing and conversing. Evette thought W*ow, this is what a perfect family is like.*

On Thursday morning, his mother took Evette to breakfast for a talk. Afterwards, they picked up Alexander's oldest sister and went to a Good Friday service. They had a wonderful time and later that night, they went to another church to support one of his older brothers as he preached there. It was her first time seeing Alexander rejoice in the Lord and it was hilarious. She was crackin' up.

The weekend seemed to move quickly and before they knew it, it was Sunday. The pastor really preached from his heart. The saints treated her very well and everyone had nothing but good things to say about Alexander. She felt even more comfortable about him as a result. When it came time to return to Mississippi, Alexander, his oldest sister, her children and Evette were at the mall. She missed her flight and had to catch another one on Monday morning.

She returned to Rollins elated. She and Alexander wrote each other often and talked long distance every day for hours at a time. People in church began to tease her about him. Some of it was humorous but most of it was sheer jealousy. She really didn't care, though.

The next time they saw each other, they were in Chicago for another national convention. That's when he proposed.

The convention was being held at the Hyatt Regency Hotel near O'Hare Airport. It was beautiful, very cozy and conveniently located near eateries and shopping centers. Evette arrived in Chicago first and called his home to let him know she arrived safely. Alexander's oldest sister, Denise, answered the phone and had led Evette to believe that he'd forgotten to get the rings. So, when the family arrived the following day, she made certain not to even bring the subject up.

She'd called her mom's oldest sister and let her know that she was in town for the convention and her cousin and uncle came to pick them up. They had a wonderful time in her finished basement watching 'Silence of the Lamb' on video. It felt as though they were in a theater. They ate junk food and drank sodas until late and then Alexander slept in the basement while Evette and her cousin slept up stairs in her bedroom. They literally talked all night long. She told her how she met Alexander and her cousin suggested that she write a book about it.

The next morning, they ate a big breakfast and spent most of the morning laughing and reminiscing about younger days. Her aunt was quite relieved to see her. She'd thought that Evette was part of a cult. She told her that she'd envisioned her walking around airports like a 'flower child' trying to sell flowers for money. Once she saw that Evette was very sane and doing well, she was happy. For lunch, her aunt made an awesome seafood & pasta salad and after she ironed their clothes for church, they were all headed back to the convention.

Service was wonderful. When it ended, Alexander and Evette went for a walk around the hotel. They found a quiet place that was off to the side of the main lobby. There was a nice, black, baby grand piano there and he showed her the chords that he knew how to play. There was also a huge, lighted, water fountain and the water poured out at different levels. They sat in the chairs and talked. Evette still didn't bring up the topic of marriage.

The next night, her last night at the convention, he had graduated from the Evangelical Training program and received his certificate as a licensed Sunday school teacher for the organization. He looked so handsome as he walked across the stage. They all wore white, ceremonial caps and gowns and it kind of made you think of what it would be like to be with all the saints in Heaven. She didn't know what everyone else was wearing under their robes, but when Alexander took his off, he was wearing a white suit, white shoes, white shirt, one of the ties that she'd picked for him on their first date and the socks that matched.

They went to what they had deemed their 'spot', sat in the chairs and talked about how wonderful the convention had been. She was wearing black pumps, sheer, off black stockings, and a silk, pink dress. She got up from the chair and sat on the side of the fountain and began to brush her left hand gently through the water. From the corner of her eyes, she noticed him reaching into his pocket. She thought *No. That couldn't be what I think it is.* She saw a little of the black ring box as he tried to conceal it in both hands. He casually got down on one knee. She still pretended as though she didn't see him. *Oh, my God! He's about to do it.* She wanted to scream!

"Evette." He said.

"Yes, Alexander." She replied.

"We've been together for quite some time now..."

"Yes, we have." She interrupted.

"And I love you very much." Alexander said.

"That's sweet, Boo boo. I love you, too."

"I know we've been talking about the will of God for us to get married and..."

"And if it's God's will, we will. One day." She interrupted again. She was still playing with the water and made it a point of not looking him in the face.

"What I'm really trying to say is." He took her hands in his. "Would you please stop playing in the water and listen to me for a second?"

She smiled at him. "Okay. I will. Not what is it that you have to say?"

He pulled out the ring box, opened it as if they were living in slow motion and said, "Baby, I love you and I can't see myself spending the rest of my life with anyone other than you. I want to wake up every morning looking into your eyes. I want to come home every day to your beautiful brown eyes and smiling face. Evette, baby, will you marry me?"

She was going to play with him and say no, but he did it so sweetly, she just couldn't ruin the moment with foolish jesting. So, with a big grin she said, "Yes! Yes! I will marry you." And they both laughed and smiled as they embraced.

"So, how do you feel?" He asked.

"I don't know." She answered.

"What do you mean, you don't know? What's going on inside you?"

"Well, I feel a mixture of emotions. I feel like running, jumping, rolling on the floor and speaking in tongues." She burst into laughter. "I just feel a whole bunch of things right now."

"Well, why don't you just do everything that you feel like doing?"

"No." She replied.

"No?" He asked. "And why not?"

"Because," she responded, "when our children grow up and I tell them about this moment, I want to be able to say that I kept my composure." They both laughed again and he walked her to her room holding hands and grinning all the way.

"Good night, baby." He said and gave me a gentle kiss on the cheek.

"Good night, Boo Boo."

She stood in the doorway and watched until he was out of sight. Then, she ran into the room to tell everyone about what had just happened, but no one was in. She was much too excited to go to bed, so she went back down to the lobby. Some of his East Coast friends were down there and they saw her coming down with a big smile.

"Oh, my God! He did it!" One of them yelled and they all came over to her. They gave her big hugs and kisses on the cheek as they welcomed her as the latest member to the East Coast crew. Of all his friends, Alexander was the first to get engaged. They stayed in the lobby until after 2a.m. laughing and talking until finally, realizing that she had a plane to catch, she went upstairs to bed. The next morning, Alexander caught the shuttle bus with Evette to the airport and saw her safely onto the plane.

When she arrived back in Rollins, all hell began to break loose as the word swiftly spread that "Evette got engaged at the convention."

Leadership Reality Check

There are really no words to describe just how horrible that year was for her. She gained new friends and, seemingly, lost all the old ones. Planning a wedding proved to be more taxing than she thought it would be. Trying to do just about everything herself could have been the main reason for that, but it wasn't because she wanted to. It was because she felt that she was left with no choice. Coming to church became burdensome because she was the topic of many a Bible Class and Sunday morning message. Everyone believed that it was God speaking directly to her through the pastor, but deep within her, it just didn't seem right anymore. And to make matters even worse, she was being approached left and right by various brothers in the church. Men who, before hand, had never given her a second glance were now asking her out to dinner. She would flash her engagement ring and tell them all "sorry, but you're too late" and yet, part of her was enjoying the attention.

One night during Bible Class, the pastor began to talk about long distance relationships and how the congregants should want to marry someone within their own flock. Evette was floored. She held her hand up and said, 'Bishop, I'm engaged.' His reply was "that ring on your finger don't mean nothin' because rings can always be given back. You never know who you're going to marry until you say 'I do.' Until then, being engaged means nothing." At that, she became speechless. All that time she was under the impression that engagements actually meant something and that night she found out differently.

Bishop began to talk to her about other brothers in the church that he felt would be suitable for her. All of them had fine jobs. All of them owned their own homes. All of them, he said, would 'sit you down' and she 'would never have to work a day in (her) life.' Out of obedience, she began to go out with some of them. Some of them were as some might say 'off the hook.' There was this one brother who lived in the country and his family owned a lot of land. He was very nice and just as demanding. Evette felt that being with him would be like being married to a schizophrenic drill Sergeant. He wanted to know where she was at all hours of the day. He wanted to tell her what she could and could not wear. He didn't like the smell of her coconut hair oil, so he demanded that she was her hair every night to avoid oiling it all together. To make matters worse, right off the bat, he told her that he wanted to have a baby every year of the marriage. Of course, he had to go. She still talked with Alexander every night and wrote letters to him at least three days a week.

The next fellow that the Bishop sent her way was very well off. He had a nice state job, owned his home and was about to purchase a second one. He was going to rent the first one out to others. His car was paid for and he believed in spoiling women. They must have dated for at least five months. He was quite a gentleman, or so she thought at the time. Al was about six feet, seven inches tall and weighed probably about two hundred and fifty pounds. He was of a chocolate complexion and had the cutest smile.

It had been a long time since she'd been consistently in the presence of a man who treated her as well as Al did. He would break his neck to open the car door for her. He was very well mannered and when he would come to her apartment, he would always sit on the other side of the room. He would pick her up from work every day. Not that she'd had asked him to, he just began to do it on his own. She actually found that to be quite appealing. After all, no woman wants a man that she has to tell everything to. After a while, it became common for them to be seen together. Some of the children of her closest friends began to tease her about marrying Al, though they stated very plainly that they wanted to see her and Jamal together.

Al began to shower her with gifts, to the point that one of her dearest friends, Shana, refused to have anything else to do with her. Above everything else, she put on twenty-five pounds and went from one hundred fifteen to one hundred forty pounds because he was taking her out to dinner almost every night of the week, especially after night services. They became close, too close actually. She began to notice that he would make little subtle moves. He would laugh and grab her hand, while saying good night and touching her cheek before walking away, stand within her personal space after having walked her to her door and always wanting to stay a little longer each time he came to her apartment.

After a while, he started talking about sex. She didn't lie to herself and pretend that she didn't enjoy it. After all, to have a conversation, you have to have at least two willing participants giving and receiving. Gradually, she let her guard down to the point that they began to kiss and make out in the car after dinner at night. Feeling condemned, she went to the pastor to confess. She told him that Al was not the person that he thought he was and that she felt as though all Al wanted was sex. Evette felt totally betrayed when Bishop, in her presence, told Al what she had said and then encouraged them to continue seeing each other.

Some would wonder, 'didn't they have their own minds?' But you have to understand the power of religious bondage and control. They practically worshipped their pastor and they never made major decisions, or casual ones for that matter, without going through him first. Evette wouldn't even visit her mother if Bishop didn't give her his approval. They were totally loyal to him. They actually feared him more than they feared God. Evette, and others as well, would often say that they didn't want to do anything wrong not because they were afraid of God but because they were afraid of confessing in extremely great detail to the pastor. They were taught to obey, obey, obey those who had the 'rule over you' no matter what. They were taught that even if the leader is wrong, you should obey, as long as it's not sin, and let God take care of the rest. It would be years before she'd learn that their mother organization was listed with the Federal Bureau of Investigation as an occult! Their founders had left the organization and began a new one because they believed that the mother organization was not strict enough. So, if the mother organization was recognized as a cult, how much more were they!

One day after work, Al was there, as usual, to pick her up. That particular day she was feeling a little depressed. It had been almost a year since she'd last seen her family and she was very home sick. She spoke to him about it and when they made it to her apartment he told her to go in and pack a couple of outfits. He was taking her home, without the pastor's permission. Though she felt guilty, she was glad to be able to see her family again.

He sat for a couple of hours talking to her mother and brother. Her grandmother came into the room, spoke, and returned to her room. Her mom told him a bunch of embarrassing stories about her child hood. Finally, he left and her grandmother returned to the room.

"Evette, don't ever be alone with that man." Her grandmother warned more than advised.

"Why?" She asked.

"He looks like the type of man that would rape a woman." And she left out of the room.

Her mom interjected. "Evette, I think he's the type that would beat a woman, so please be careful. I know you're going to do what you want to do, but just be careful of him."

"But mommy, he's saved." She said.

"Save or unsaved, niggahs are still niggahs. Remember that."

She had a wonderful weekend with her family and friends and when Sunday evening came, Al was right there to take her back to Rollins. He actually started calling her mother 'mom.' She was polite, but Evette could tell it pissed her off.

Instead of going to church that night, they went to an isolated place to talk. He began to talk to her about all of the things that he'd done for her up to that point and began to kiss her. He told her that he even wanted to learn how to apply relaxers so that he could start doing her hair. The more he talked, the more he kissed and the more her body responded. Half an hour later, her skirt was up and he was trying to penetrate her. It had been so long since she'd had sex until it hurt too badly to keep trying. Since he couldn't even get the head in, they had oral sex. This was the first of many times to come.

Evette still kept in contact with Alexander and she continued the plans for their marriage, but she felt herself spiraling downward.

Though she became a walking manifestation of guilt and condemnation, Bishop seemed pleased that she and Al were getting along so well. Evette decided, after several months, to cut it off. That's when she saw the side of him that her mother warned her about. The night that she spoke with him and told him that he wasn't good for her spiritually, he raised his hand in anger and for a moment she felt as though he was actually going to hit her. The next day, she was serving in the fellowship hall after service, and he came up to the Bishop's table and made a scene. Thank God there were other brothers of the Waiters and Waitresses Committee who were able to steer him away before he became out of control. He actually pointed his finger toward her and shook his fist. She thought to herself *and this is the man that Bishop wants me to spend the rest of my life with. I don't think so!*

The year of the wedding was a very difficult one. Bishop had no problem with her marrying Alexander; he just wanted them to live in Mississippi instead of Maryland. She had served in all but two weddings in the church in the five years that she was there and yet, when her turn came, she was having problems finding help. One person flat out told her no. Three of her bride's maids dropped out because they said they felt as though she was 'getting married just to have sex without condemnation.' Her response was, "If all I wanted was sex, why would I marry a man who is a virgin? If sex was the reason, it would seem logical for me to marry someone who is just as big a freak as I am."

She continued to be the not-so-subliminal subject of Bible Classes and Sunday morning messages. One morning, a visiting Evangelist was preaching and he began to talk about long distance relationships and how they are not God's will for His people. He said that God would give you a spouse that's in your midst. Everyone who sat anywhere near her in the choir stand began punching her in the back, hunching her shoulders and telling her 'God is talking to you. You'd better listen. Don't you marry that brother.' Every time something like this would happen, she would rush to the pay phone in the lobby after service, call Alexander and cancel the wedding. Days later, it would be back on again.

One Sunday morning, there was another visitor who'd been allowed to preach and like those who came before him he included something about long distance relationships in his message. Afterwards, while serving at the Bishop's table, Evette overheard the Bishop say to the man, "That's the sister I was telling you about who is going to marry someone all the way in Baltimore, Maryland."

From that point on, Evette began to doubt everything that came out of Bishop's mouth and the mouths of others regarding her relationship with Alexander. She began to see that Bishop was not God and that not every word spoken from the pulpit was 'a word from the Lord.' This hurt her more than anything, because at that time, Bishop was like a father to her and she trusted him. She lived, like others, according to his dictates and that moment caused her to question everything that she had been taught by him. She felt stupid. She felt as if she had believed the hype and that maybe everyone was right all along, but she still could not bring herself to leave. The church had become her safe haven, her source of peace, her escape from the cares of the world and she depended upon it even though she wasn't totally living by its standards. Evette had become 'churched.'

She wrestled day and night with an inner struggle that, until this point, she'd never known before. What do you do when you can no longer fully trust the word of a man that you, at one point, entrusted your very life to? If Bishop had told her to slap the President, she would have found a way to Washington and knocked the President unconscious. Now the man that she would have done anything for became a tool of the enemy in her eyes and the 'attacks' became increasingly open and humiliating.

One Friday night, during a Saint's Meeting, Bishop had asked her to stand up. That in and of its' self was embarrassing because generally during Saint's Meetings people were kicked out of the church as punishment for their sins. However, he wasn't carrying a manila folder.

"Sister Evette Williams, would you please stand up?" He said with a stern look on his face. A hush fell over the church. There had to be at least two thousand people there that night. Though the church could comfortably seat approximately thirty-five hundred, only those who had been baptized in Jesus' name and who had also received the Holy Ghost (as evidenced by speaking in tongues) were allowed to attend Saint's Meetings. Some people actually put their hands over their mouths and looked as though they were about to start crying. Others smiled as if to say, 'it finally caught up with her.' She stood as she was told, trembling and holding onto the pew in front of her. She always sat in the second seat of the second row, so everyone in the building had a clear view of her.

"Most of you know that Sister Evette is engaged to a brother from Baltimore. I want you to pray...."

"Bishop!" She interrupted with a shout.

He looked down upon her from the podium. "There's nothing wrong with praying, is there?" He smiled and asked.

She dropped her head. "No, Bishop. There's nothing wrong with praying."

He continued. "I want you all to pray that if it's God's will it will not happen." He looked back at her and said, "You may be seated."

After service, people came to her smiling and saying, "We're going to be praying for you. You're not going anywhere." "God is trying to help you. You'd better let him."

At the next Saint's meeting, Bishop opened up a manila folder and silence fell across the church again. Everyone knew that if Bishop came into the sanctuary for Saint's Meeting carrying a manila folder, someone was about to be disfellowshipped. In church, the worst possible thing that could happen to you was being disfellowshipped. It was a fate worse than death. At least death frees you from the cares and people of this life, but when you have been excommunicated from the saints, it plays on your mind and often breaks your spirit. There are some that feel they have no hope left in God when it happens. They were taught that in this process, your soul is being handed back over to the Devil and you cannot come back into fellowship with God until the pastor who disfellowsipped you accepts you back. Though the Apostle Paul speaks of it in I Corinthians, it should be the exception, not the norm and it was a punishment for the unrepentant so that they could repent. It was not to be used as a means of control and manipulation. Moreover, once the person repented, Paul advised that they be immediately received back into fellowship. So, Saint's Meetings, to Evette, were like attending the funerals of the living dead. Like most funerals, there are always three groups of people who show up - those who cry and wail over the loss; those who seem happy to see you go; and those who just came so they could leave with gossip about the ones who cried and the ones who cared less.

He asked a sister to come up to the pulpit and stand before everyone. She was crying and obviously embarrassed. Evette wept for her. She seemed so broken and distraught. Evette knew her. She had been born and raised in the church all of her life. She was a virgin and a straight A student. Bishop went on to tell the congregation how she came to him and told him that she had been on campus returning some books to a resident in the girl's dorm. On her way back to her car, she was snatched into a car by several guys, was taken away and gang raped. Her first experience with sex. He told the church that she said she was too embarrassed and hurt to go to the hospital or to tell anyone in church. Everyone remembered how suddenly her behavior had changed but no one knew why, until that night. Now, she was pregnant.

"What was she doing on campus alone at night in the first place? She wanted something to happen to her." One brother in front of Evette said.

"Are you crazy!" She shouted. "She is a student. The last I heard, campus grounds are usually the place where you'll find students. No woman wants something like this to happen to her. What would you say if she was your sister? Your mother? Your wife or aunt or cousin!" She demanded more than asked.

"I would say don't go out at night alone unless you're looking for trouble?"

Bishop put her out of the church and said he was making her an example to other young women who might think that they could go out, fornicate, get pregnant and cry rape. He said that 'if' what she said actually did occur, he would be praying for her. He proceeded to tell her that she could not have an abortion because that would be adding sin on top of sin. Months later, she gave birth to a son.

The last time Bishop asked Evette to stand before the congregation things went a bit differently. It was a Sunday night and the church was full.

"Sister Evette, would you please stand?" He asked. The church became quiet. "Sister Evette will be getting married in a few weeks and she will be leaving us. She is a hard working, dedicated sister and she has faithfully served in this ministry." The people agreed. "You slow brothers let this sister walk around here for how long?" He looked at her.

"Five years, Bishop." She said.

"Five years. And not one of you snatched her up. Well, God told me to tell you that you missed your blessing."

For the first time in almost two years, she felt at ease. She actually exhaled and smiled. Then a week before the wedding, he told her that he would not be giving her away. She was hurt but she understood why. He knew that although she loved Alexander, she wasn't in love with him and that would make a difference.

As the weeks approached, a lot of things transpired. The night before the wedding, she was having difficulties obtaining enough time for the rehearsal. It seemed that Bishop was throwing monkey wrench after monkey wrench in the way. He tried to talk her into having it in the small sanctuary on the other side of the building. It was nice, but it was extremely dark and small. Then he complained about the way some of the ladies were dressed and tried to lead her to think that God was insulted by them being in the church with shorts on. Evette reminded him of all the Jimmerson State University students who had come to church in their attire and eventually got saved.

They had to rush threw the rehearsal and Alexander's brother had to rush threw her song. One of the bride's maids had written a song for Evette to sing while coming down the isle. Alexander's brother was able to grasp the song in the fifteen minutes that they had and even then, they cut the lights out in the sanctuary.

By the time she got ready to leave the church, she was beyond frustrated. She had no one to serve the food, and no one to clean up afterwards. Despite Bishop's announcement, he left out the part that she had his blessings and because he didn't publicly say it, the people felt that though the men in church had 'missed' their blessing, Bishop was against her marriage.

"Evette, are you all right?" One of Bishop's nephews asked.

"No, actually I'm not all right. I cannot believe that I have been working and serving in this church faithfully for five years, serving in everyone's wedding, including yours, giving my money when all I had to eat for months was bologna, crackers and water and this is how you all treat me! This is what happens to people who try to leave?"

"Don't worry about it." Her coordinator said. "Tomorrow everything will be fine."

Three of her best friends from high school, one of which was a maid of honor, along with her sister, wanted to take her out. However, because they were not 'saved' Evette was taken to one of the church mother's homes for the night. They said the reason was because she had a 6:30a.m. hair appointment and they wanted to ensure that she didn't miss it. She must have gotten about two hours of sleep that night because every time she turned over she was in the bathroom throwing up.

She got her hair done and started running around tying up loose ends. She still had some packing to do, mostly the gifts she had received during her lingerie shower. As she picked up the items and put them into the suitcase, she reflected back on that night. Only eight sisters came and most of them were part of the bridal party. She was hurt. She truly was. However, she thanked God for those who did come and tried hard to maintain a brave front.

They had played games that she was remembering with a smile. They were all asked to write her name, Evette, on top of their papers. Then they had to think of as many Bible characters as possible for each letter of her name. For example, 'E', Enoch, Elizabeth, Ezra, Esther, etc. She had everything video taped so as the years passed she'd be able to pull it out from time to time and watch it. It amazed her that she went from having fifteen bride's maids to three and from two maids' of honor and two matron's of honor to only two maid's of honor or NO matron's of honor. She went from having nineteen ladies to only five, but she understood why. They lived their lives by the Bishop's words and his failure to speak actually spoke volumes.

"By the power invested in me by God and the State of Mississippi, I now pronounce you husband and wife. You may salute your bride."

Alexander lifted the veil that shielded the face of his new bride and smiled. He took her in his arms, bent her back and laid one on her!

Responses came from the crowd. "Wooow!" "You go, boy!" "That's enough, let that girl breathe!"

The wedding was supposed to begin at 3:30 but Bishop had them to start of 3p.m. Thus, there really weren't a lot of people there and by the time they showed up, it was over. Because the wedding party was so small, the entire thing took about half an hour. Bishop kept his back turned on Evette and Alexander as they passed by him to light the candles.

"Ladies and gentlemen may I present to you the new Mr. And Mrs. Alexander and Evette Worthington." People began to gather around and embrace them. "Treat her right, you hear." "Don't forget to come back and visit us sometime girl." "Yeah, especially after you have your first baby." "You two look so beautiful together." "This is the best wedding I've ever been to."

Cameras were flashing all over the place. She felt like a movie star. She had been a faithful member of the church for five years and she was told that her presence was going to be missed. She'd been a member of the adult choir, and was one of the directors. She was assistant director for the youth choir, and the head director of the children's choir. She was on the waiters and waitresses committee, the baptismal committee and the tarrying committee. She was an actress in the church's drama guild. On her days off, she volunteered at the church helping to clean up and assist in the office. She'd served and helped prepare food for every wedding held at the church since she'd become a member. She was editor of the church's newsletter, entitled 'The Messenger'. It had become a lucrative project for the youth department, as various businesses placed ads within it. Finally, she was a member of the missionary department and a youth counselor.

Her major weaknesses were that she talked too much and she was hooked on sex like an addict on crack. She had to have it. Until that day she had managed to never cross the line. She usually ended up masturbating.

Alexander was a born and bred Baltimorean. Unlike Evette, he was raised in the church from the womb up. He was about five seven, of a slender build, brown complexioned with very wavy hair. He had dimples and could sing your socks off! At his church in Baltimore, he was one of the associate ministers, president of the young people's department, director of the adult choir, and faithfully cleaned the church on his days off, too.

People took turns during the reception expressing their sentiments on the video. "Alexander," said Juanita, "I want you to know that you're not just taking a sister away from me, you're taking away my best friend." She took a deep breath and let it out. "Well, I guess I'm not going to have anyone to trip out with now. 'Cause couldn't nobody trip out with me like Evette. You know how some saints can be."

A young man, Charles, stepped next to her. He was smiling. Turning up her nose and looking at him with sheer disgust, she said, "Get him away from me. I don't want him on this camera with me." And he left. "Well, God bless you both. By the way," she threw up her hands, "I missed the whole thing. I got here late. Yours *would* be the only wedding in the history of the church to start on time. Well, that's it. I'll miss you girl. Don't forget me."

Next was Minister Abraham, with his preaching tone of voice. Everyone considered him to be very phony. "Well brother and sister Worthington, God bless you on your new endeavor. And sister Evette, remember what the Bishop always taught, submit and obey. You obey him, not the other way around." Juanita, overhearing him, steps back up, rolls her eyes, and says, "Man, ain't nobody trying to hear that."

He looked her up and down and said, "Sister Evette, *you* know what the Bible says. And with that, God bless you." He looked back at Juanita and said, "And you wonder why you're almost thirty and still single," and walked away.

Though there were about sixty or more people at the ceremony, the reception was packed. Like most occasions, people came and brought their kids so they wouldn't have to cook dinner when they went home.

The reception was beautiful. The colors were black, white and tea rose. All the tables were draped in white tablecloths with black runners down the center. Long stemmed tea rose candles sat on every table in the center at every third seat. The plates were also black, white and tea rose. Tall, white, Greek pillars surrounded the dining hall and they were all spirally draped with sheer material that was tea rose. Artificial white doves hung from various parts of the ceiling. Everything was beautiful.

"A toast" said Justus, the best man and all glasses, which were filled with punch, were lifted. "To Alexander and Evette, a match made in Heaven. May your marriage be filled with all the blessings that any one couple can handle. And try not to have too many babies." Laughter filled the room as they clinked their glasses. "To Alexander and Evette!" Everyone shouted.

Dinner was served. The menu consisted of honey-glazed chicken breast; cubed, skinned potatoes in a butter and garlic sauce; homemade rolls; tossed salad; spinach dip with Jewish bread; cake; mints; nuts; and punch. Evette and Alexander took pictures while feeding each other cake and sipping punch from 'bride' and 'groom' glasses.

"All right! All right! May I have your attention, please!" Yelled Denise, the maid of honor. "It's time for all single young ladies ages 18 and up to catch the bouquet." Women came running from everywhere. "Over here Evette." "Girl, don't nobody want you. Evette, right behind you, girl." Evette raised the bouquet high, all hands went up and she faked them all out. The men laughed, as some of the women fell on the floor trying to grab what they thought was a toss. The men knew what the women had obviously forgotten that the first was always a fake one that was done for the sake of the photographer. The second time, Evette made sure she tossed in the direction of her dear friend, Antoinette from high school. "Ha! I got it! Thanks girl!" All the other women were pissed and walked away rolling their eyes.

Next, she sat in a chair as Alexander reached up her gown to get the garter belt. She couldn't help blushing because he caressed her thigh. "Wooow!" came the cheers and applause. One man yelled, "She's all yours now man, you can touch her anywhere you want. Anywhere you want." Evette smiled and shook her head while Alexander laughed.

When the single men finally gathered, after being beckoned several times, hardly anyone tried to catch the garter. As it flew through the air, they turned their backs and walked away. Kind of like the waters that Moses parted. It landed on a young man that wasn't paying attention and he dropped his head and said, "Aw man!" The other men pointed and laughed at him.

They went around bidding their farewells and then she went to change into her going away outfit. It was a T-length, peach, two-piece, silk outfit that was trimmed with designer studded lace. She went into the sanctuary to say goodbye to the choir. They were preparing for a concert and had decided to keep rehearsal scheduled after the reception. When she entered, everyone stopped singing and began smiling and saying goodbye. She went over to Bishop, and kissed him on the cheek.

"Goodbye Bishop. We're off."

He looked at her with a deep sadness in his eyes and gave her a hug.

"What's the matter, Bishop?"

"When you get to Baltimore and see that things are not what you thought they would be, come home."

"Bishop. Don't you want me to be blessed?" She asked.

"Of course I do, but there's a lot that family isn't telling you. I'll give you three months, not even that long and it's all going to fall apart. When it does, come home."

She walked away.

When she made it to the van, everyone was already loaded and ready to go. All of the young girls she'd counseled, encouraged, prayed with and let live with her when their parents kicked them out, were gathered outside. They all cried and kissed each other's cheeks as they gave one another their final hugs. Gwen and her newborn twin boys were there also. She was the first person that stayed with Evette when her mom had kicked her out. Gwen had wanted to be saved, but her mom put her out because she viewed the church as being an occult. Now here she was, two years later, married and with children of her own.

Evette hopped in the van and they drove off. After they passed through North Carolina, Alexander told her that they were not going to have a honeymoon. She was deeply disappointed, especially since Alexander had contributed nothing towards the wedding, reception or picture expenses. He'd had a full year to save, but he didn't do anything. He also let her know that he'd quit school. He only had two years to go and he would have had his Bachelor's degree in Architecture. Her head was spinning, but it was too late now.

Five hours later, they arrived in Baltimore in front of his mom's house. They all said good night and he pointed her to the church's 15-passenger van and said, "Get in."

"Where are we going in that thing?" She asked.

"Home." He replied, as he began taking her things from the trunk.

"What happened to your car?"

"It got towed. Come on, let's go."

They climbed into the van and drove to their two-bedroom apartment. It was pretty nice to say a man lived there, but she knew it could stand a woman's touch. The carpet was your traditional beige. The living room furniture was plaid but it was Broyhill. The dining room furniture was a six chaired, oblong glass table set. One bedroom, the smaller one, had only a twin set of mattresses on the floor in a corner. The master bedroom contained a three-piece, black with gold trim bedroom set.

She only had a few suite cases. She had to leave the bulk of her things in Mississippi because nothing else would fit. It was 98 degrees on the day of the wedding, but when they arrived in Maryland, it was 76. All of her winter clothes were to be picked up in December.

She went in the bathroom first. She brought her green overnighter in with her because it was filled with everything she'd prepared for that night. She ran a hot scented bubble bath, climbed in and bathed with the scented soap that matched; *Lilly of the Valley* by Victoria's Secret. When she finished drying herself off, she lotioned her body with the final piece of the collection. The scent filled the hall. She pulled out her negligee and began watching herself in the mirror as she put it on. It was one of the gifts she'd received during the bridal shower. It was white lace and very sheer, a costly piece of apparel. It was embroidered with beautiful white jewels and fell half the length of her thighs. She smiled with approval at her reflection, put on the matching robe and white fur covered slippers and exited the bathroom.

"Are you finished?" He asked.

"Don't look at me," She said as she dashed into the second bedroom. "Just go on in the bathroom and take your bath. I'll be waiting for you."

While Alexander was running his bath water, she locked the bedroom door and kneeled down beside the bed to pray. She'd been taught that sex within the context of marriage was a holy and sacred act. Also, that God himself anointed it and smiled from Heaven whenever a couple celebrated its rites.

She was nervous. "Father, I'm coming to you tonight as I make ready to consummate my vows with my husband, Alexander. Holy Spirit, please come into the room and fill it with your anointing. Jesus, please cleanse the atmosphere and make it pure. Bind every spirit of perversion that might try to interrupt and cheapen our experience together." She heard the bathroom door open. "In Jesus' name. Amen."

She quickly unlocked the door, hopped in bed and tried to appear as sexy as possible. It had been five years since she'd last indulged and her body was yearning for him. Unlike Evette, Alexander said he had never experienced sex before. She was to be his first and only.

He entered the room in his briefs and smiled at her as she lay on the bed with one arm behind her head and one leg propped up in the air. *Are those the same underwear?* She thought. He slowly approached the bed, as if savoring every moment that was a part of this experience. He gently took her in his arms and they began to sensuously kiss. Since she was more experienced, he let her take the lead and she made love to him. She began to cry and worship God. It was the most beautiful encounter she'd ever had. She actually started speaking in tongues. Alexander couldn't believe it. When it was over, they held one another and talked.

"Are you sure you're a virgin?" She asked.

"Well, I'm not now." He laughed.

"No, are you sure I'm the only woman you've ever been with?"

He kissed her forehead. "Yes. You are and you were indescribable. It was better than anything I could ever have imagined. Why do you ask?"

"Because you weren't acting like it was your first time."

"I wasn't?" He seemed almost offended.

"No. You seemed as if you've done this before."

He smiled again. "I guess it's like they say. Instinct picks up where experience leaves off."

He'd taken that entire week off from work so that they could be to themselves, or so she thought. They were in church every night. When St. Andrews wasn't having services, they went to other places. They never got a chance to bond, except when they were in bed having sex, which soon became all the time.

Bishop Phillips' brother, Marcus, had given her some pre-marital advice before she left Mississippi. "Up there," he said as he pointed to her head, "has nothing to do with down there. It's your duty to please your husband whenever he wants it. Remember, your body is no longer your own. It's his. So handle your business or someone else will."

Evette handled her business all right. They were averaging sex fifteen times per week, and that didn't include weekends. It not only had to do with what she was told, she loved sex and also, they were trying to conceive.

Alexander had married her knowing that she had a severe case of endometriosis and was not supposed to be able to have children. When Evette discovered the news, she went to Bishop Phillips and he advised her that Alexander had the right to refuse to marry her if he wanted children and she wasn't able to give him any. But Alexander told her, "I'm not marrying you for what I can get out of you. I'm marrying you for who you are."

Her period was late for the third time and, again, they were hoping she'd conceived. Alexander went out and purchased a pregnancy test. After she urinated on the stick, they sat in the bathroom watching and waiting to see if the second red line would appear. It didn't. He held her in his arms as she broke down and cried.

"Baby, don't worry. God's going to bless us in his own time. Just wait and see."

"I know. It's just that I feel abnormal. Like I'm less than a woman. I'm not asking for the impossible. All I want is to be able to give you a baby."

He continued to hold her and let her cry until she was ready to let go. Then there was sex. Sex was his way of trying to fix things.

DURING

Down Hill From Here

It was Monday morning, December 13. A day she was to remember for the rest of her life. That Sunday, the pastor, Elder Michael Bogess, told her that in January she'd be preaching her trial sermon. She was elated. She'd been awaiting her release into the ministry for years and now she was literally standing on the brink of it.

That morning, she saw Alexander off to work and began to pray and read her Bible to seek the Lord for what He would have her to say. She felt led to preach about the crucifixion of Jesus; how he was rejected back then and how people today, in the church and out, are still rejecting him. As the words began to flow across the paper, she heard the buzzer sound off. She ran and looked out the window to see Marvin, one of Alexander's younger brothers standing there. *Why isn't he in school*? She wondered.

She yelled out the window. "Is something wrong? Did something happen at the house?" No response. She buzzed him in. While he was climbing the stairs, she asked again, "Is everything o.k. at the house? Why aren't you in school?" Again, no response.

They entered the apartment and he closed the door behind them. "Have a seat. I need to get dressed." She left him in the living room and went into the bedroom. She was wearing a white slip and her husband's navy blue robe that was trimmed in burgundy. She closed the door behind her and tried to decide what to put on. She pulled out her favorite. An Elizabeth Claiborne 2-piece set. It was red, with white polka dots. As she laid the outfit on the bed, a strange feeling swept through her. She turned around and was startled to see Marvin standing there in the doorway watching her.

He glanced at the bed. "That's a nice bear you've got there."

"Yeah. It was a gift." She threw it to him. "You can look at it in the other room."

"You have some nice cassettes, too. Mind if I put something on?"

"No. Go right ahead. You can play whatever you like. Try the one by Keith Dobbins and the Resurrection Mass Choir. It's their latest." He left the room and closed the door. He had the music blasting.

Moments later, he burst back into the room and threw her on the bed. She began screaming and trying to fight him off.

"What are you doing? I'm your brother's wife! Please don't do this to me!"

She wrestled her way off the bed and he threw her on the floor. He kicked her in the side and she doubled over as spit flew out of her mouth. He jumped on top of her and threw the robe over her face. She felt his fingers as he jammed them up her vagina.

"Oh, God! Please, help me! Jesus, please help me!" She was screaming at the top of her lungs, but the sound of her cries only blended in with the music.

She felt a sharp object. "Shut up before I cut you! I swear to God, I'll cut you!" But Evette kept screaming and she kept fighting. Suddenly, she began to hyperventilate. It scared him so badly; he jumped up off of her. He thought she was dying. That gave her enough time to leap up and run out of the room. He chased her around the dining room. She faked him out to the left, took a right and ran into the kitchen. From the drawer, she grabbed two butcher's knives. He came behind her and grabbed the knives, his arms wrapped around her. She snatched the blades through his hands and his blood splattered on her slip. He ran into the living room. She followed and held the knives toward him.

"You get the hell out of my house! You hear me! Get the hell out!" But he stood there with a smug, almost sadistic look on his face.

"You can't kill me. You're in the church." He said, and laughed.

"What?" She was totally taken aback. "What? I'm in the what? Niggah, you're in the church, too. Hell, you were raised in the church!"

Seeing that he was not about to leave, she did. She ran screaming and crying down the stairs and into the street with the knives waving through the air. It was cold and she was bare foot and wore nothing but the blood stained slip and Alexander's robe.

An African American male saw her running. He flagged down an elderly white couple who helped her in their car and took her to Elder Bogess' house. Elder Bogess was their pastor, but he was also Alexander's uncle. They blew the horn and he came out. They helped her out of the car. She was still screaming, crying and shaking all over. The pastor helped her in the house. Aunt Margaret ran down the stairs.

"What in Jesus' name is all this racket going on down here!" She saw Evette. "Bogess, what's going on with this girl?"

"Marvin tried to get a hold of her." She looked at Evette.

"Child, why did you open the door?" But Evette was still hyperventilating and couldn't respond. Aunt Margaret's question only served as an unwelcome additive to her pain, because she made it seem as if by opening the door, it was Evette's fault. She helped Evette upstairs and into one of the spare bedrooms.

"Bogess, where are you going?"

"To check on Denise and see if he went by there to bother her and to go check on Evette's apartment. She left everything open. Just tend to her, Margaret and call Sister Worthington. I'll be back."

Denise was Alexander's oldest sister. Later, Evette learned that Marvin had tried to rape her, too, but he did her far worse than he did Evette. He beat her in the head with a two by four. The family swore her to silence because they didn't want to tarnish their name, but some things have a way of letting themselves out of the closet.

By the time Evette got control of her breathing, Denise burst into the room screaming and apologizing.

"Evette! Oh, Evette! I'm sorry. I'm so sorry. Oh, God, I'm sorry. I should have warned you about him. I'm so sorry."

She embraced her. They cried together as Denise rocked her back and forth in her arms. Elder Bogess entered the room.

"I don't care what the Devil tries to do, God *is* going to be glorified. Hallelujah!" He clapped his hands three times and left out. Evette could have spit down his throat.

Somehow, she managed to fall asleep. When she awakened, she was taken to Denise's apartment where she got in bed again. By now, all of her muscles were aching and she could barely move.

Back at Edith's house, Alexander was in the process of hearing the news. It was about 7:30p.m. He climbed the steps behind his mother. Donald, his brother that was under him, was talking to Marvin in the hall. Alexander was the last one to hear about what had happened to his new bride.

"Alexander, sit down on the bed, son."

"Mom, is something wrong?" He could see that she'd been crying.

"Yes. But before I tell you, I want to ask you a question." He looked at her with a confused expression on his face. "Are you saved?" She asked.

"Mom, what kind of question is that?" He was appalled.

"Just answer me, son. Are you saved?" She was really serious.

"Yes, ma'am. I'm saved." Alexander answered.

"Are you sure you've got the Holy Ghost?" She just kept prying.

"Yes, ma'am. I'm sure. Where is all of this going, mom?" He was becoming agitated.

"This morning, around 10a.m., Marvin went to your home, beat and tried to rape your wife." She quickly threw up her hands and added, "But he didn't and she's all right. She's at Denise's house and we're about to go over there."

"Did you say this happened around ten this morning? Mom, it's almost 8p.m. Why didn't someone call me earlier?

"Well, son..." He interrupted.

"Obviously someone called you. Does Donald know? Is that why both of you were acting so strange on the way home? Jesus Christ! I don't believe this! My wife is assaulted by my brother and I'm the *last* one to find out about it!" He jumped up from the bed and placed his right hand on his forehead and shook his head.

"Now, Alexander. Remember, you said you were saved. What would Jesus do? Remember, you said you were saved."

He broke down and began to cry. All of his life, he'd been taught not to fight, but at that moment, all he wanted to do was beat the hell out of his brother.

"Remember." She added. "Greater is he that is in you then he that is in the world. You still have to remain godly even when faced with ungodly situations. This is just a trick of the devil to divide the family. Furthermore,"

"I want to see my wife." He demanded as he cut her off.

"Okay. Let's go." She picked up her coat.

They left the room. He passed Marvin but said nothing. Alexander, Donald, and their mother drove to Denise's. Once there, they discovered that Latonya, her husband Leland, and John, the youngest brother, were already there. Their mother was the first to enter the room. She knocked on the door.

"Who is it?" Evette asked as she was awakened by the knock.

"Evette. It's me, momma. Can I come in?

"Yes, ma'am."

She entered and sat in a chair beside the bed. She held Evette's right hand between both of hers and let out a deep sigh.

"I want you to tell me exactly what happened." Evette told her every detail. She left nothing out.

"Uh! Oh my God, Evette. You cursed."

"What? I just told you that your son tried to rape me and all you can focus on is the fact that I cursed! Where's my husband?"

She called Alexander into the room. Again, she had to tell the whole story over as he sat on the bed holding her hand and her mother-in-law sat in the chair listening. When she finished, Edith got up, wiped the tears from her face and left them to be alone. On her way out of the door, she turned to Evette and said "The Bible says we're not supposed to take our brethren to the law." Then she asked. "Are you still blessed?"

Evette looked up at Alexander and said, "I want to go to church tonight."

Surprised, he asked "Are you sure you wanna do that?"

"That's all I know to do. Besides, if I stay home alone the only thing I'm going to do is think about it and cry." She let out a heavy sigh and added, "I wanna go home, Alexander. I don't think I can handle coming to church every day and seeing your brother."

"It's not God's will for us to leave Baltimore."

"How do you know that? Did HE tell you?"

"No. My mother has been telling us all of our lives that it is God's will for the family to be together. I know some of us have left, but they'll be back." She left the subject alone. They hugged one another and exited the room.

Denise had already gone to their apartment and gotten her a change of clothes. She took a shower there and got dressed. It was the red outfit with the white polka dots. As they came out of the bedroom, all conversation ceased. Donald stood there staring at her. The rest joined in.

"Evette wants to go to church." Sighs of relief filled the air. They were afraid she'd want to press charges.

Latonia smiled nervously and said, "Your wife is smart. Very smart indeed."

They all left and headed to the east side of Baltimore to Faith Temple where Elder Bogess was to be the guest speaker. Praise and Testimony service was already in progress. They were singing...

"What a fellowship. What a joy divine. Leaning on the everlasting arms..." Evette stood up and Alexander's family dropped their heads.

"Praise Him, Sister Worthington," said the young lady who was leading the services.

Evette was in so much pain and her muscles were so stiff, she had to prop herself up by using the pew in front of her. Tears began to stream down her face.

"I will bless the Lord at all times and His praise shall continually be in my mouth." Denise and Edith began to cry. "I want the devil in hell to know that I *will* bless the Lord at all times and his praise! I said his praise! Shall continually be in my mouth!" And she sat down and worshipped God in spite of the trauma, in spite of the pain.

The next day, she woke up in a bed full of blood. She cleaned herself up, put on a pad and ran to Denise's apartment. Denise drove her to the clinic. She couldn't believe it. She and Alexander had been trying so hard to conceive and now this.

"Denise, if I was pregnant and he caused me to lose my baby, he's a dead man."

Denise sat in the corner, rocking and crying.

"God won't let you be pregnant. He'll cover both of you."

"I really don't care if God protects your brother or not."

Thankfully, the results were negative. They also performed tests for HIV and other sexually transmitted diseases as a precaution. All tests came back negative. Denise sighed and said, "Thank you, Jesus."

When they made it back to the apartment, Donald, Latonya and their sister from Michigan, Malika were there.

She had to cook and serve them. By her being from the South, it was almost expected. Good thing Evette loved hostessing anyway or else they would have been in for it.

Being a closely-knit family, they all sat huddled together and spoke only to one another.

"So Alexander, how are *you* enjoying the married life?"

"So far, so good. How are things with you and Kenny?"

"Oh, great. We're about to start pastoring a church of our own soon."

Denise interrupted. "I'm surprised he let you come, girl."

She was shot a look from everyone and she quickly changed the subject. The Worthington's were a very secretive family. Part of what bonded them was the fact that only they were considered 'the family.' The in-laws were a separate entity. This, too, was made obvious when they spoke.

"Donald, what do you and Alexander think about all of us having family prayer every Monday night?" asked Latonya.

Donald responded. "I think that's a great idea. We can pray for the unity of the family…" Alexander interrupted.

"And we could also pray for God to continue to anoint us in ministry."

Latonya continued. "Yeah, and if the in-laws don't like it, they don't have to come. It will just be the members of the family."

Evette served quietly. When finished, she ate her food in the kitchen and then went in the living room and watched television, alone. Her heart yearned for home.

Three months went by. One night, they were at church. A visiting preacher was ministering. When he'd finished preaching and had changed clothes, he said, "While I was in the back, God showed me that there is a couple in this church that has been trying to conceive." He was looking directly at Evette as he spoke. "I want you to raise your hand or I'll come and point you out."

Evette raised her hand slightly so no one could see. She was on the front row. He smiled at her and said, "I knew it was you. God said to tell you that it's already done." She began to cry and worship God.

That night, she and Alexander went home and made love. Two months later, she still wasn't pregnant.

"Baby, I think you should take the test."

"I don't know, Alexander. I'm tired of being disappointed." She was packing boxes, preparing to move. "Every time I've taken a pregnancy test the results were always negative."

"I think you should. Entertain me. Just this once."

She let out a deep sigh. "O.K. but only because you insist."

He walked up the street to Harris' Fine foods and purchased a home pregnancy test. He stood impatiently in the line waiting his turn. It was the beginning of the month, so all of the lines were filled with women whose baskets were overflowing. It was an hour later when he returned. His breath was labored because he ran all the way back and up the stairs.

He looked at Evette and smiled but she dropped her head and proceeded to unwrap the pregnancy test. She went into the bathroom and urinated on the stick. Later, she returned to the bedroom and in their usual fashion, they both sat together and waited to see if the second line would appear. The package said it would take less than five minutes, but within moments a pink line appeared. The longer they watched, the darker it became. Finally, it dawned on them that she was actually pregnant this time.

Evette began to cry as she lifted her hands in worship toward God. Alexander began to jump up and down.

"God, I thank you for healing me. Thank you, Jesus, for this miracle child."

"Yes! Yes! I knew it!" He said as he wrapped his arms around his wife. "I knew you were this time! Thank you, Jesus!"

And they settled down for a dinner of spaghetti and meatballs. In the back of her mind, she was petrified. Most women have the pleasure of having their moms present, especially when they are going to give birth to their first child, but her mother, her whole family, was over a thousand miles away. Reality hit like a cold winter slap of Maryland wind.

"Evette," said Kelly, a member of their church, "Where are you guys going to be moving to?"

Evette mustered up a smile. "The Lord knows."

"What does that mean? The Lord knows?"

"It means that I don't know but HE does."

"I bet you never thought you'd come all the way to Baltimore and go through something like this." She said as she shook her head and walked away.

Under her breath, Evette whispered, "No, I really didn't." But here she was 2 ½ months pregnant with her first child, over a thousand miles away from family and friends, homeless and without medical insurance. She began to regret the day she even met Alexander.

He'd proven to be nothing of what she expected. She guessed that's what happens when you're involved in a long-distance relationship. She felt as though she should've waited, especially after she'd learned that Love had divorced his wife.

He was her one true love. She fell in love with him when she was 18. He, too, was a born and bred Mississippian. He was her first real date - about six weeks after she'd graduated from high school. Though he was a year younger, he was definitely more mature. He was about 5'11" and weighed about 150lbs. Very intelligent and could speak fluent Spanish. He was perfect in every way except for one flaw. There's always one flaw. Love had a bad temper and although Evette seemed to bring it out of him from time to time, she still loved him dearly. He was the only man she'd ever been willing to put her life on hold for.

So, here she was, married to one man and deeply in love with another. She'd adjusted herself to the grim thought of having made her bed hard. Now, she just had to deal with it.

"Lord," she whispered a silent prayer, "Give me strength and get the glory." She was interrupted by a knock on the door.

"Evangelist Worthington, are you ready?"

"Yes. I'm coming." She exited the pastor's office and was escorted to the pulpit. Praise and Testimony Services were still going on and the congregation was singing. 'I've got the Holy Ghost down in my soul, just like the Bible says. I've got the Holy Ghost down in my soul, just like the Bible says. Well, I've been to the water and I've been baptized. My soul got happy and I feel all right. My hands got stuck to the Gospel plow. I wouldn't trade nothin for my journey now. Oh, just like the Bible, just like the Bible, just like the Bible says.....'

She took a deep breath and kneeled down to pray. When she finished, she took the seat that she was directed to take. She was dressed in a red and white maternity suit with matching red pumps. Latonia had regretfully given it to her. She didn't want to give it to her, but her stomach was bigger than Evette's and she didn't want to throw it away. There was about two week's difference in their due dates.

When praise service ended, Alexander was asked to sing a solo. He chose, 'It's my desire.' Afterward, Pastor Bogess introduced Evette.

"Praise the Lord, Saints! It is an honor as well as a privilege for me to introduce a young sister who is an anointed, powerful, woman of God. She is originally from Mississippi and as all of you know, she is the wife of Minister Alexander Worthington. She's packed with the word, so I know we're going to hear something tonight. Saints, visitors, friends, and enemies too, if you're here, give a hardy hand praise for Evangelist Evette Worthington and say 'Preach the Word! Preach the Word! Preach the Word! In Jesus' name!'"

The sanctuary thundered with applause. She stood up, took a deep breath and thought, '*Lord, please bless me not to pee on myself.*' She smiled and stepped up to the podium. Silence fell across the room. She opened her mouth and began to sing.

"I've had some good days." *She thought about her wedding.* "I've had some hills to climb. I've had some weary days." *Flashes of her assault and attempted rape came to her mind.* "And some lonely nights." The tears began to flow. "But when I look around and I think things over, all of my good days outweigh my bad days" *She really didn't mean that part.* "So, I won't complain." And the anointing of God fell. When she'd finished the song, she felt the strength to move forward.

"If you would open your Bibles to the book of the Psalms. Chapter 41, verses 5 through 11. Shall we all stand in reverence to the reading of the word of God?" The congregation stood. "If you would be so kind as to read along with me. And the word of God reads as thus....*Mine enemies speak evil of me. When shall he die and his name perish? And if he come to see me, he speaketh vanity. His heart gathereth iniquity to itself. When he goeth abroad he telleth it. All that hate me whisper together against me. Against me do they devise my hurt. An evil disease, say they, cleaveth fast to him and now that he lieth he shall rise no more...'* We'll stop there. No, let's read verse 11. *'By this I know that thou favorest me, because mine enemy doth not triumph over me."*

"Look at your neighbor and say, 'they left me for dead.' The congregation repeated. "But I got up!" Cheers rang through the air. She began to nod her head and smiled as she made eye contact with the people. "Uh hm, *they* left me for dead, *but* I got up! As a companion scripture, I'd like to use St. Luke, chapter 10, verses 30 through 37."

"Has anyone ever left you for dead? Has anybody ever looked at your mistakes of the past, judged your present and condemned your future? Has anyone ever looked at the lives of your family and friends and condemned *you*? Has anybody ever looked at you and said 'you ain't nothin. You ain't never gone be nothin. Your daddy ain't nothin and therefore you ain't gone be nothin either!' Has anybody ever left you for dead?

"Here we find David in a predicament of extreme proportions. He has sinned. Not only has he sinned, but he contracted an STD in the process. To add to his woes, the folks he thought he could trust the most, after he confided in them, put his business in the street! Have you ever gone to the one person you thought had your back and found that they had it all right, with a knife! Because of his condition, they said 'oh, he got over the last test, but he's not coming out of this one. This one is going to take him out of here. He ain't gettin up.'

"Sometimes, you look for help from the folks sitting in church right next to you every week and find none. Jesus told a parable of a man who fell among thieves. Sure he was alone walking in a dangerous part of town and should've known better, but how many of us have found ourselves in situations where we should've known better? And the Bible says that the thieves had left him for dead. Now, one would think that the Priest and the Scribe, or in modern terms, the Pastor and the Teacher, would've stopped, but they didn't. They were too busy. After all, they were heading to the synagogue. How many times do we miss opportunities to minister to people because we're too busy going to church to try to reach the folks that already know what we're talking about anyway!"

Cheers, claps and laughter rang trough the sanctuary. People could relate.

"Oh, but the one who stopped! The one that stopped to help the man was the one considered to be an outcast. He was a Samaritan and Jews were not supposed to have any dealings with people from Samaria because they were half-breeds. There were half Jewish. But honey, when your life is at stake, you'll forget about your racial divides. You won't care if the person is black, white or blue. All you'll want to know is 'can you save me? Can you help prolong my life just a little while longer?'

"Look at your neighbor and ask 'em, '*can you save me? Or will you pass me by and let me die?*" They repeated. "Get an answer! Get an answer! But also let 'em know, '*if you don't, God will send somebody else.*' Because, baby, when it's not your time, it's not your time. God will raise you up like he did Lazarus. Like he did Jairus' daughter. Like he did the only son of the widow! God will! God will! Raise you up!"

"But what are you going to do when you get up? David continued on as being the greatest king Israel ever had. He continued in his purpose. The man on the side of the road? Well, we don't hear anything else about him. The same holds true for Jairus' daughter and the widow's son. Lazarus, however, went on to continue serving and following the Lord. The one thing that they all had in common was that at a future date, they all died again. So what are you going to do now that you've been given another chance to live? Are you going to wait until the next thing comes along that could possibly take you outta here? Or are you going to make good use of your second lease on life, be it natural or spiritual, and fulfill your destiny? I know what I'm going to do. So how about you?"

When she sat down, another minister approached the altar to make the water call. Before he could open his mouth, droves of people flooded the altar. Some were crying and repenting, others were praising God, but they came. Those who were seated began to sing a hymn entitled "Love lifted me." Evette bowed her head and whispered, "Thank you, Jesus." The church's atmosphere was electrified. It was six months overdue, but years from now, Evette would recall her trial sermon as being the most unorganized she'd ever preached.

When service ended, people came from all directions hugging and kissing her.

"Praise God Evangelist Worthington. The Lord really used you today." Another older sister said, "Sister Worthington, if you keep going like you're going, one day, God will make you a great Evangelist"

Evette thought to herself, *'One day?' Shoot, I already am! Was she asleep or what! They loved me. I can do this preaching thing with my eyes closed. Heck, I don't even have to study.'* But instead she said, "Thank you, Mother Bailey.

Keep me in your prayers." She smiled and was suddenly whisked away by Sister Bogess, the Pastor's wife.

"Ya'll get out of this Sister's face. You phony, hypocritin demons! Get away." She pushed passed the congregation members and took Evette into the office so she could change.

"Evette, you ain't got no business calling yourself tryin' to preach like that and you're pregnant. You need to be somewhere sitting down. I don't know what's wrong with Alexander. He needs to stand up and be a man and put you in your place!"

"And how do you propose he does that? Aunt Margaret, you really need to mind your own business and stop being a busy body in other people's matters."

"Why you old snake-spirited demon! I'm the pastor's wife. How dare you talk to me like that!"

"Aunt Margaret, if you'd please excuse me, I really need to get changed."

She stormed out of the office and slammed the door. Evette took a deep breath, let it out in frustration, shook her head and said, "That woman would make the Devil in Hell pray for deliverance."

Aunt Margaret approached Alexander. She was wearing a full length, navy blue, double-breasted skirt suit with a cream blouse, navy blue pumps, a scarf that was unnecessary and a gold 'I love Jesus' breast pin. Aunt Margaret was very light complexioned, heavy set, but not fat, and was said to have been the cause of most people having left the church. She had a stank attitude.

"Alexander!"

"Yes, ma'am Aunt Margaret."

"Come hear! Let me tell you something."

"What is it? Is something wrong?"

"Yes. It's that demon you married."

"Demon?"

"Your wife. Don't play with me boy. You know who I'm talking about."

"What about Evette?"

"You treat her too nice. You need to be hard on her."

"What?"

"You need to keep her in her place. If you don't crack down now, she'll run over you later. You better listen." And with that said, she stomped away, leaving Alexander standing there with his mouth wide open.

Aunt Margaret had a way of dehumanizing people. By the time she got finished with you, all you wanted to do was go curl under a rock somewhere.

As time passed, Evette grew bigger and bigger. Some people in church had hurt her feelings by telling her that she looked as though she was pregnant with twins. They didn't have much money, so she was hungry all the time. She hated it the most on Sunday mornings because Alexander drove the church's van. Quite often, they left out without having had breakfast. If she asked for something to tide her over until dinner, which was served every Sunday around 4p.m., she was met with disdain. All she ever wanted was a 25 cent pack of peanut butter crackers and a bottle of apple juice, but Alexander's family told him that it was just a trick of the devil to get him out of the services. So, out of obedience to them, he wouldn't go.

She learned to cope with her hunger by falling asleep in church. There were times when she felt as though she'd faint because she was so hungry, but no one seemingly cared. They told Alexander often, that *"She's from Mississippi. She's strong. She can handle it."* But they went off when Latonia's husband didn't get her something to eat and it resulted in her fainting in the middle of their church.

She wanted to return home but was told that the only person she'd be hurting was Alexander and he hadn't done anything to her. But actually he had. In failing to support, protect and provide for her, he had hurt her more than any of them could. Much to her dissatisfaction, she stayed. Not so much because she loved him but because she hated to fail and wasn't the type that enjoyed hearing people say 'I told you so.' To add to matters, they were both now in ministry and how would it look to the world if the God who created all that was, is and will be in six days, who hung the sun, stars, and moon in place, who can keep a fish in salty water without the fish tasting salty itself, can't keep one Christian marriage together? Even if it was a mistake. So she stayed.

It was a few weeks later when she learned of the conversations Aunt Margaret had been having with Alexander. They were at his mom's home when she called.

Evangelist Worthington passed him the phone. They were in the kitchen.

"Alexander, telephone."

"Who is it, mom?"

"It's Aunt Margaret. She heard your voice in the background and asked to speak with you. Just take the phone and be nice."

He let out a deep sigh. "Praise the Lord, Aunt Margaret. What can I do for you?"

Everyone stood around him watching his smile fade as it was replaced with a frown.

Evette demanded, "What is she saying to you?" But his mother, Edith, hushed her.

"Goodbye Aunt Margaret. God bless you, too."

"What was she saying to you?"

This time he told her. "She was just saying the usual stuff. That I treat you too nice. I'm not mean enough. That's all."

"That's all!"

Edith interrupted. "Now, we don't want to get carried away. Remember, you're still saved. What would Jesus do?"

Evette looked at her and frowned. "What would what? What would Jesus do! I'll tell you what Jesus would do! He would go over there, lay hands on that busy body and cast the devil out! That's what Jesus would do, and I think that's what I need to do, too!"

"Now Evette, somebody has to be the example."

Evette looked over at Alexander. "Is that why you've been treating me so badly?" He said nothing, but dropped his head. "That's low, Alexander. Why couldn't you have followed the advice of the people who were telling you to treat me right, and work hard for your family? I wish I'd never met you at all."

"Now Evette, you don't mean that." She glanced at her mother-in-law with a sharp, soul-piercing look and stormed out of the kitchen.

"Alexander, go after her. And make sure she doesn't call anyone."

He got up to leave and then turning, he looked pitifully at his mother and said, "I always thought it was right to obey you all, but now I see that you truly do not have my best interests at heart."

"Now son, don't let the enemy talk to your mind. That's just the devil trying to bring division into this family." She put her hand on his shoulder. "He'll use whomever he can. Don't let him use you." She walked out.

Alexander took another deep breath. "Women aren't the only ones who are waiting to exhale."

Marriage Ministry Seminar

"First of all, I want to thank all of you who pressed
your way out today. I'm always glad when saints come out
in spite of the weather. It lets me see who the real saved
people are." Chuckles were heard through the sanctuary.
It was Bishop Langley from D.C. He was the Diocesan
Bishop for the East Coast Holiness Churches within the
organization. He was about 6'11" and could be described
as 'well fed' by his wife. Bishop Langley was an
extraordinary man. Very well versed in the Bible, he was
an excellent Preacher, Teacher and Counselor. He was at
St. Andrews that Saturday to teach a marriage class. As
was his usual method, he began by passing out surveys for
all of the couples to anonymously fill out. It contained
questions such as, "On a scale from 1 to 10, with 10 being
the highest, how would you rank your marriage?" Evette
and Alexander, unknown to each other, both wrote 4. "If it
was not totally against the will of God, financially feasible,
and not a total embarrassment, if you could, would you get
a divorce?" Evette checked 'yes' while Alexander checked
'no.' Everyone finished answering the questions and began
to turn their papers over. Hearing the sound, Bishop
Langley looked up.

"If you're all finished, you can pass your papers to the
person sitting at the end of the row and I'll come around
and collect them."

Everyone did as they were instructed.

"By the way," he added, "please be respectful of one
another's privacy by not looking at people's responses."

He collected the surveys and scanned through them
briefly as he occasionally nodded, smiled or frowned. Then
he looked up at the awaiting crowd of 20 couples.

"You know saints, I've been facilitating marriage
seminars for over 15 years now and it never fails to be
confirmed that those who have good, positive responses on
their surveys are those who've been married the least

amount of time. Say, one year or less. After that, the marriage really begins." There was a moment of nervous laughter. "After about a year, unfortunately for some, after a couple of months, or even more unfortunate, during the honeymoon, things change." People began to shift in their seats.

"How many of you have heard of P.M.S. as it relates to marriage?" All hands went up. "I'm not talking about that uncomfortable thing women experience during certain times of the month, though that does affect marriage. I'm talking about *Power, Money and Sex.*" They sat up in their seats as an indicator that Bishop Langley had their full attention.

"That's right. Power. Who is in control? Though we all know what the Bible says, the man is indeed the head, the leader of the family, sometimes because of human nature lines may become blurred. Who wears the pants in the home? Who has the final controlling word?" The men began to smile and sit upright.

"Since the bra burning Women's Liberation Movement of the sixties, women have launched an all out campaign aimed at dethroning men from their rightful, God-given roles as leaders in the homes, in the work place, in the world at large." Some of the women began to twist their lips at that last statement, but not one of them dared to open their mouths in verbal protest.

"And what was the result? No fault divorce, broken families, higher crime, higher instances of unwed pregnancies, abortion. Anytime we step away from the order of God, the end result is always chaos! Wives, you married that man. Whatever he may or may not have been or whatever he may have developed into, when you said 'I do', you chose, at that very moment, to place yourself under complete and total subjection to that man. He is the head. He is the authority. His is the final word. As wives, your duty is to reverence, obey and submit."

The room suddenly became over-crowded, not because more couples came in, but because the chests of the men that were there became so big it was almost claustrophobic.

"However" he continued, "There is more to being the head then going around barking out orders as you pound your chest. You are to lead by example. Give your wife something worth following. Your job is to love, lead, provide for and protect. If the truth be told, you have the toughest job with the greatest level of accountability. When something goes wrong, we tend to blame women, just like Adam did, but God puts the burden on us. He holds us accountable for the breakdowns of the family.

Suddenly, you could breathe again. The men's chests went back down to their normal sizes and the Bishop continued.

"Has anyone ever wondered why the Bible never says that wives should love their husbands but it does command the husbands to love their wives? Not with any ole kind of love either. It says to love them 'as Christ loved the church and gave himself for it.' That's powerful! My brothers, if you will love your wives as Christ loved the church, she in return will automatically submit. She'll automatically reverence you."

Someone interrupted. It was an older man who looked as if he could have been in his fifties. He was tall, lean, very handsome and had peppered hair.

"What about 'obey', Bishop? You didn't say anything about that."

"That's because the Bible says they are to obey 'as it is fit in the Lord.' So, she's not obligated to obey your stupidity. You don't give someone a dumb command and expect them to obey it. See, if you are loving her as Christ loves the church that means you'll be fasting regularly. You'll be praying daily and seeking the face, the will, as well as the hand of God. And if you're doing what you're supposed to be doing, all of what you ask of her will be God-led, God-centered, and God-like. Notice, nothing is about you. Everything is about God and about you being led by God. When the Jesus in her sees that you are being led by the Jesus in you, automatic submission and reverence occurs."

"On the other hand, the God in her is not going to be subjected to the devil in you." He began to pace. "Moving right along. The second thing that affects marriage is money. This doesn't have to be a problem when there's enough or so one would think, but it is, especially if the wife is making more than her husband. If he's not a mature fella, secure within himself, he can and will actually become jealous and give his wife a hard time in an attempt to show her that he's still the boss.

For instance, both work 40 hours or more per week. The husband comes home and sits in front of the television or computer and there he is until it is time to eat. The wife, on the other hand, comes home from work and heads straight to the kitchen to cook. This is followed by her doing the dishes, helping the children with homework, getting them prepared for bed and finally settling down herself. All this while the husband was doing nothing; and he has the nerve to *expect* her to have sex with him as tired as she is knowing they both have to get up for work the next morning. And some of you get mad if she doesn't feel like it and have the nerve to try to make her feel guilty by quoting scripture. Shame on you."

"The flip side of this coin can be when the wife makes more money and the husband becomes deflated by her constant flaunting of it. Sisters, that's just wicked and if you're doing it, you need to stop. How can you expect your husband to rise up to be the man God created him to be when you are consistently emasculating him? You are actually short changing yourself."

"We should have the attitude that it's all going into the same pot, because it is."

A sister interrupted this time. "Excuse me, Bishop. I understand that everything is supposed to go into the same pot, but what if your partner keeps putting a hole in the pot and all the soup is being wasted on the floor and the whole family is going hungry as a result?" She seemed a bit perturbed. Her husband dropped his head.

"Then you have your name taken off the account and open a separate one in your name only. You don't sit back and let your family go under. Do what you gotta do that's pleasing to the Lord, and handle your business. At the same time, sit and talk to your spouse and let him know that you're not disrespecting his headship, but as his help meet, it is your responsibility to help see that the family doesn't die. Do it in love, not with an attitude and pray for him. Let him know that you will be standing in the gap and praying that God will take him to the level of headship that you know he's capable of being."

"Now, the third side of money is the most common one, not having enough. You work hard, you pay your tithes and offerings, but you just can't seem to make it through. This is the time when you and your spouse have really got to be on one accord."

A hand went up. "Well, Bishop what do you suggest about spending habits?"

"I would suggest that you two consult each other before making even a $15 purchase. That goes especially for the husbands because often our wives have to come to us if they want a $2 pair of stockings but for some reason we have it in our minds that we can do as we please. That's very unwise."

Bishop got up from the table and began to pass out papers with questions about the couple's sex lives.

"Again, please do not sign your names to these surveys. Reason being, I want you to be totally honest." There were a few giggles. "I know, saints don't lie but we'll sho'll 'nuff leave out details that would change the entire meaning of a thing." They laughed.

There were questions on the survey that went into great detail about intimacy in marriage. Such questions as, 'on average, how many times do you and your spouse have sex per week?' 'Do you practice oral/anal sex?' 'When a disagreement occurs, is sex used as the method for making up?' 'On a scale from 1 to 10, with 10 being the highest, how would you rate your sex life?' 'If your sexual needs could be met by someone else, without the fear of going to Hell, would you commit adultery?' 'How do you feel when sex is over?'

Since there were no names requested on the survey, Evette answered, *Ten times per week. No oral/anal sex. Yes, sex is making up. I would rate it a 4. Yes, I would have my sexual needs met by someone else. When sex is over, I feel like a toilet that has just been used and flushed.*

Bishop Langley collected the papers. He was astonished with the responses that he glanced through. He'd been facilitating these seminars long enough to know which papers belonged to the wives. He stood up, walked over to the chalkboard, picked up a piece of yellow chalk and drew a large curve. Then he picked up a piece of white chalk and drew an upside down V. At the top of this diagram, he wrote the words *Sex of the Sexes.*

"This is the most sensitive area of marriage other than power and money. He said as he looked seriously at the couples. "Who would you think the long curve represents?"

One by one, with great pride, the men said the big curve represented them. Evette blurted out, "The large curve represents the female and the sharp curve represents the male. Both lines depict the rate of sexual satisfaction, orgasm, and the rate at which each comes down from an orgasm."

"That's right, Sis. Worthington."

The men got pissed.

"That's exactly right. There is a huge difference between men and women when it comes to sexual arousal and gratification." He pointed to the sharp lines. "Men get aroused very easily. It doesn't take much for a man to become erect and want sex. A good looking, half dressed woman can walk in here right now and I guarantee, as saved as we think we are, no matter how many tongues we speak in, at least ½ of the men in here will become erect."

"On the contrary, let a half dressed man come in here and most, if not all, of the women will think, *'Now he knows he needs to go put some clothes on.'*" The women began to laugh and nod their heads.

"Women are aroused by thought and sound not sight. They can remember a romantic encounter and become excited. That's why they are not the ones making pornography the multi-billion dollar industry that it is today. When it comes to making love to your wives, brothers, you've got to remember that it takes women longer to get there than us, especially if you've done or said something to upset her or hurt her feelings. While you're humping away, the only thing going through her mind is what you did or what you said."

A hand went up. "Bishop, may I ask a question?"

"Sure you can."

"When is the best time to start getting them revved up?"

"The best time to start is in the morning and not when your penis is up before you are. When you wake up, give her a kiss on the neck. Stroke her hair gently with your hand as you pass by her and smile. Tell her how beautiful she looks and how much you love her. Sing to her sometimes. Since women are turned on by sound and thoughts, give her something to think about all day. Call her just to say 'hi' and to see how her day is going, especially if she's home with the children all day or has a highly stressful job outside the home. If you don't, someone else surely will."

He continued. "Take her out to dinner. Have a bouquet of flowers delivered to her. If your finances don't warrant you the opportunity to afford such things, get a colored piece of construction paper and make a homemade card with an original poem. That will mean more to her than receiving a *Hallmark*."

All the women started nodding, smiling and clapping.

"Brothers, I'm telling you, if you do these things, you'll have some peace. You can take that any way you want." They laughed.

"And sisters, it's your turn. Will y'all stop going to bed in hard curl rollers and flannel night gowns." The men started clapping. "For God's sake, please stop! You complain about how your husband is not romantic anymore. He doesn't make advances towards you any more. Well, how is he supposed to get in the mood when he goes to rub his hands through your hair and can't because of those big ole pink things? By the time he gets finished raising up all that flannel stuff and going through cotton drawers, he's tired. So all he can do is roll back over and go to sleep." They were all laughing at this point.

"I guarantee you one thing, that other woman ain't crawling into the bed smelling like bleach and Pine-Sol and wearing something that would turn Stevie Wonder off. You've got to do things, Godly things, to keep the fire burning. Don't give him any reason whatsoever to get what I call 'The wandering eye disease.'

A hand went up. It was Aunt Margaret. She had just walked in. "Bishop, excuse me please, but could you answer one question for me?"

"Yes ma'am, go ahead." He responded.

"Should your spouse go out and make purchases that you don't agree with?"

Everyone let out a sigh because they knew she was throwing off on her husband for just having bought a new Lincoln Town Car behind her back.

"No. Men, I don't care how much of a man you think you are. The Bible says that a house divided against itself shall not stand. Yes, you are the head. You are the leader, but you have to exercise wisdom. You have to remember that marriage is a joint venture not a dictatorship. Decisions should be made with mutual consent, especially if you're having financial problems. I would recommend that you don't even spend as little as $15 without mutual consent, and if she's better with handling finances, let her.

It doesn't take away from your manhood or headship to allow her to do that."

"A wise man knows how to delegate authority. Only a fool would know that he's not good at handling money and continue on anyway. It's just down right of the Devil! You're sitting back and allowing your family to suffer over your sinful pride. And you wonder why God hasn't blessed some of you."

"That's why I admire successful men so much. If you ever notice, when they achieve a level of success, they give credit to two people, God and their wives. Poor men have only themselves to accredit. Ain't it funny that you don't find many successful women that can say that they are where they are because of the help of their husbands? Usually women have to be successful in spite of us not because of us. That shouldn't be so, my brothers. That should not be so."

"And sisters, don't get the big head and think you can treat your husbands any kind of way just because he's smart enough to give you his permission to handle the funds."

A hand went up. It was Alexander's. "Bishop, should a couple study the word and pray together?"

"A family that prays together stays together, but that doesn't mean it has to be hand-in-hand. I like to pray around 6a.m. by the bedside. My wife likes to pray in the middle of the night in the study. We pray at different times and in different places, but we're still praying. After 30 years, I'd say we're still together and in every sense of the word."

He stood up. "Proverbs says that a wise man hears instructions but a fool goes on and perishes. If you want your relationships to perish, go on as you've been and it will happen just as sure as there is a Devil in Hell. However, I would that you be wise and allow God to mold your relationships into the image of the relationship between Christ and the Church."

They applauded as Deacon Harvey gave him the envelope that contained his honorarium.

"Shall we all stand and be dismissed?" Said Deacon Harvey. "With uplifted hands, may the words of my mouth and the meditation of my heart be acceptable in thy sight. Oh, Lord, my strength and my redeemer. In Jesus' name, amen."

Months later, changes could only be seen in two of the couples that had attended the marriage seminar. Eventually, both couples left the church to go to places where family wholeness was emphasized.

Kitchen Talk

Alexander walked into his mother's living room and took a seat on the couch. Evette quietly tipped upstairs to lie down in the computer room.

God, Alexander thought, *please help me. Open a door for us.* His thoughts were interrupted when his father entered the room.

"Praise the Lord, Alexander."

"Praise Him, dad."

"What are you dong sitting in here by yourself? Where's Evette?"

"Oh, I'm just meditating. Evette is upstairs resting."

"It's almost that time isn't it? She looks like she could pop any day now." He laughed.

"Yes, sir. Actually, she can go any day now. She's already dilated three centimeters."

"Humph. Ain't that something? Well, I'm going upstairs."

"Good night, dad." He watched him tip up the stairs and then he heard his bedroom door close. *Same ole dad always tucked away in his room.*

Though Alexander loved his father dearly, he couldn't help but think of how neglected they all felt as young men growing up in the world. They had lived a sheltered lifestyle that consisted mostly of going to school and going to church. His father worked all the time. He had to, to take care of a wife and nine children. They despised him for it. When he would come home, he'd go upstairs, close and lock his door. He never spent quality time with them. He never talked with them about the things that boys need their fathers to talk about such as sex, girls, wet dreams, and what it means to be a man and a leader in your home. In short, he never invested in them and because of it they grew up with an abundance of God, but lacking in all other areas. They depended upon their wives to help them mature into the men that they had the potential to be.

One thing could be said about Elder Worthington, though; he gave them all that he'd been given; God and nothing else. I guess he figured that if you have God, He'll make up the difference of whatever else is lacking. He failed to realize that despite the fact that his sons needed God, they also needed a father and bringing home money to pay the bills doesn't constitute being a good father. Sure, its better than being a dead beat dad, but what children, especially African American youths, need is someone who will pour life into them and be a good example.

"Alexander!" It was his mother, Edith, calling him from the kitchen.

"Yes, mom?"

"Dinner is almost ready. We're having left-overs."

He hated having to eat over there every day, but what could he do when they were just getting back on their feet after having been laid off? Evette thought he enjoyed going to his mom's, that he loved being around his family. The truth was that's all he'd ever known to do, be secluded with his family. From his youth, they were taught to stick together and leave outsiders where they were, outside. Besides, Evette had a habit of talking too much and when a person is talkative, they tend to let unmentionables slip.

His family, though they smiled in Evette's face and called on her whenever they needed help with something, couldn't stand her. They thought she wasn't good enough to bare the Worthington name and had even told her to her face. After all, she wasn't raised in church like they were. She wasn't a virgin when Alexander married her, like most of them were when they got married. Finally, she had no musical abilities. She couldn't sing unless someone taught her the part and even then she'd often change keys.

Alexander thought about the positive things about her. Evette was the kindest person he'd ever met. She was caring and giving and as much as she loved to talk, she was also a good listener and the best friend anyone could ever have. She always went the distance for those she cared about. She was long suffering with the faults of others, but she was hard as hell on herself. She wasn't quick to judge people and always tried to see the good in even the most wretched. Though she didn't have what his family considered talent, she could teach and preach circles around most of them and she was truly anointed. His family looked at her and saw her for what she used to be. He, on the other hand, looked at her and saw what she would become-an awesome woman of God. He smiled at the thought of how her gifts could be used to grow his family's ministry.

Evette sat upstairs playing solitaire on the computer. It was difficult to rest with the children running around and coming in and out of the room. She kept clicking new game until she came across a hand that had a somewhat even amount of red and black cards. She played, half-heartedly though, because she was thinking about the turn her life had taken. Tears began to roll down her cheeks. Maryland was not what she had envisioned. For over ten years, Baltimore City's homicide rate had been over 300, making it one of the most deadly cities in the United States to live in. Here she was, in her first year of marriage, pregnant with her first child, over 1,000 miles away from everyone she knew and loved and to top it all off, homeless.

After Alexander had been laid off in the middle of the worst blizzard that Maryland had seen in 15 years, they lost everything. They found themselves staying with whichever members of the church would open their doors to them. Now they were finally staying with his oldest brother Benjamin, his wife and their three children. They were finally able to start saving their money. Everyone else that they'd stayed with had charged them so much money they could hardly buy food let alone save for a place of their own. No one wanted them to stay with Benjamin and his wife, because he was a backslider and his wife was a sinner, but they had been more of a blessing to them then those who had claimed to be holy and sanctified. *Kind of makes you wonder sometimes*, she thought.

She remembered Bishop Phillips' last words to her that day of her wedding before she left for Baltimore. *When you get to Baltimore and see that it's not what you thought it would be, come home.* She shook her head at the thought. She couldn't bear hearing almost 3,000 people saying 'I told you so.' She whispered a prayer as she wiped the tears from her face. "Lord, please bless us."

There was a knock on the door. It was Edith, her mother-in-law. "Evette, dinner is ready."

"I'll be down in a minute." She went into the bathroom and washed her face. When she came into the kitchen, plates were being fixed. All the children and the grandchildren were standing around watching as Edith fixed their food. This was a ritual that Evette hated. *How can they all just stand around and let her serve them like that?* She thought.

"Evette, what do you want on your plate?"

"You don't have to fix my plate." She said as she pulled a plate from the dishwasher. "I'm old enough to serve myself." And she shot a cold look around the room. The others lowered their eyes, but no one attempted to serve themselves.

It was a simple dinner of string beans, spaghetti and meatballs. You could always feed a crowd with spaghetti. Though most of them went into the dining room to eat, Evette remained in the kitchen. Edith remained with her.

"Evette, how have you been doing?"

She twirled some spaghetti around the fork and looked up. "I think you know how I'm doing, but to answer your question in a way that's least confrontational, I'm blessed."

"Evette, I'm trying to get along with you."

"Are you? Are you really? You tell me I'm not good enough for your family. You tell me I'm not musically inclined. You only treat me nice in public when you're tying to maintain a certain image or when you want me to help you do something. Now that all of these walls are built, you want to 'get along'. I'm sorry, *Evangelist* Worthington, but there are some people that you just can't pick up and put down at will. People have feelings, you know."

"Baby, I'm sorry. I know we've judged you and have dealt with you unfairly, but can't we please start over?"

"Where would we begin? I mean, so much has happened. I just don't know how or where to begin."

"Let's start from this moment on."

Evette glanced at the book her mother-in-law was reading. It was lying on the counter of the kitchen island. *'Biblical Examples of Women in Loveless Marriages and How They Coped.'* She dropped her head and thought, *why is she reading something like this?* She looked up at her mother-in-law who, to her surprise, was already staring at her. Edith got up and began to wipe the counters.

"I never told you about my childhood, did I Evette?"

"No ma'am. You never did."

"I've just finished T.D. Jakes' book, *Daddy Loves His Little Girls*. It helped me to not only understand myself, but to also understand you."

What is she rambling about, Evette thought. "Oh, really?"

"I think I'll let you borrow it." She pulled it from the shelf above the refrigerator and handed it to her.

"Did you know my father was an alcoholic?"

"No, ma'am. I didn't."

"Yes, he was. He was quite a mean man. Beat my mother terribly." She said as she shook her head. "He seldom brought his money home. Everything he made, he'd drink away, but my mother loved him something fierce and was determined to make it work. Back then, 'for better or worse' really meant for better or worse, not like these days. Nowadays, people have no regard for commitment. Instead of trusting God to hold things together, they look for the first sign of escape."

She continued. "He was tall and handsome. Looked just like my brother Jim. My mother was of a chocolate complexion. Beautiful. She had a smile that could penetrate the deepest pain and make it go away. And could sing! She had a strong alto voice. It was so strong, you could here her clean across the fields of the County. During school hours, kids would let the windows up and listen to my mother sing hymns."

Evette sat listening. *Why is she telling me all of this? Is she really trying to bond with me after all the things we've been through?*

"I was the oldest girl out of six children, so I was responsible for a lot of things around the house. I would help cook and clean. Sometimes, when there was nothing to eat, my mom would have me set the table anyway, and she'd pray and pray and pray. It never failed. God always came through for us. There were plenty of times when my uncle would go through white folks' neighborhoods, pull food from their trash and bring it home to us. My mother would wash it off real good, if it was meat, and we'd eat it, but only during summer. Momma didn't believe children should eat meat during the school year. She said it dulls the brain."

Evette began to understand how it was that she could eat food that had been sitting in the refrigerator for days without giving it a second thought. She guessed that was a delicacy compared to eating from someone else's trash. She sat up and began to see her mother-in-law in a different light.

"God saved me when I was ten years old, and shortly afterwards my family began to get saved. By the time I was finished high school, Brother Worthington and I got married. We were taught that after high school, education was a waste for women because the only thing you'd ever do was stay home and raise babies. You didn't have to have a degree for that. So most of the women in church married young and sure enough, almost every year we were expecting." Edith had been taught that it was wrong to say the word 'pregnant' and would cringe when she heard someone else say it.

She went on. "I had never seen a naked man before and the sight of him made me run outside, sit on the porch

113

and cry. And when our first baby came," she shook her head, "the only thing that helped me was the thought that Eve had to deliver her first child alone too." Evette frowned trying to figure out what she was talking about. Edith continued. "You see, back then, they didn't allow men to be in the delivery rooms. So, I was all by myself."

"Evette, do you know what it's like to get tired of living and decide to die?"

"You mean suicide?" She asked. Her mind flashed back to her botched attempts.

"No. Just being tired."

"No ma'am. I can't say that I do."

"That's what happened to my mother. One day she said she was tired of suffering and wanted to be with the Lord. So, she went upstairs, lay down in her bed, went to sleep and never woke up."

Evette interrupted. "May I ask you a question?"

"Yes."

She picked up the book about loveless marriages. "Why are you reading this? I thought things were fine with you and your husband?"

"Everything glitterin ain't gold."

"May I read it?"

"Why? Alexander loves you."

"Humph. He has a strange way of showing it."

"You have to remember, he was raised in church all of his life. He's not experienced. You're the only woman, other than those of us in his family, that's ever been in his life in any way. I think you can allow a certain amount of time for growth. After all, just like you, he's never been married before."

"You're right. I have been rather hard on him, but the Lord is blessing and.."

Alexander entered into the room while she was in mid-sentence.

"Baby, are you ready to go? Benjamin and his wife are here to pick us up."

"Yes, I'm ready." She gave her mother-in-law a hug and headed out. "Good night."

"Good night. You all be careful, it's raining pretty badly out there."

Alexander caught his mother's glance and lagged behind a bit as Evette exited the kitchen.

"Yes, mom."

"Make sure she doesn't talk too much with Stacy."

"Yes, ma'am."

"Son."

"Yes?"

"You know I love you and I want to see you happy. I only want the family to stay together."

"I understand, but you have to realize that 'the family' includes the spouses as well. You can't expect them to feel good about being isolated."

"I know. That's why I'm getting closer to Evette. She's the one that can do the most damage."

"How so?"

"She has nothing to gain or lose. That makes her dangerous to us, especially if she finds out the real secret. Understand?"

"Yes. I don't agree, but I do understand."

"Good."

"But mom, remember, some things have a way of letting themselves out of the closet." And he walked off.

Edith sat there, sipping her mint tea. Then she took the last gulp, looked at the kitchen door and said aloud, "Not if I can help it."

I think it's Time

They sat in the back of Benjamin and Stacy's 1991 Impala. Evette was tired. The baby was now six days past its due date and she was more than ready to get him or her out. Alexander held her in his arms as she rested her head upon his shoulder.

"It's about that time, ain't it girl?" Stacy asked.

"Yes. In fact, I'm almost a week over due."

"Oh, girl, you're fine. They always say that you can go two weeks before or after the date that they give you. I know you've got to be tired though."

"I'm beyond tired."

They pulled in front of a Cherry Hill row home. At that time, Cherry Hill was one of the worst places in Maryland to live. It was overflowing with drugs, gang violence, and robbery. You name, it was there. Evette thought it somewhat reminded her of Cabrini Greens, one of the most violent projects in Chicago, Illinois. Drug dealers were hanging out on the corners selling without regard to or fear of anyone seeing them. Up the street, they were finishing the parking lot of a new apostolic church whose pastor was promising to revitalize the community for Jesus and the Lt. Governor was talking about her new idea called 'Hotspots.' This, she promised, would target the most vulnerable areas around the State of Maryland and hopefully decrease crime.

Stacy showed them upstairs to the oldest girl's room. That night, Evette washed and braided her hair and they all sat in the family room and watched television.

"Aunt Evette," said Sandra, their youngest child.

"Yes, baby."

"Is it time for the baby to come out of your stomach yet?"

"Yes, sweetie. It is."

"Oow, Aunt Evette," said Delaine, the middle girl, "Can I touch your stomach?"

"Ooow, me too." "Please."

All of them wanted to feel the baby move and she obliged them all.

"Sure you can. Come on. The baby is moving right now."

"Oh, man. I feel it." "Move, let me feel it." "No, my turn, my turn."

Stacy interrupted. "That's enough. Get off Aunt Evette's stomach before you hurt her."

"Aw, mom."

"You heard me. Now, go to bed. You have to get up for Sunday school in the morning."

They all headed up stairs.

"I think I'll call it a night, too." Evette said as she made her way towards the steps. Alexander followed. They got undressed and attempted to take a shower together. She felt awkward because of how big her stomach was. Alexander dried her back and helped her put scented lotion on her body. He put on a plaid pair of boxers and she put on a white negligee that had wine colored flowers trimmed in gold. They got in bed. Alexander was fast asleep but Evette was restless. No matter what she did, she couldn't get comfortable. She wasn't in any pain, but something told her that it was time.

Around 6:30a.m., when everyone was downstairs preparing for Sunday school, she came down smiling. They all looked at her wide-eyed because she was holding her stomach.

"I think it's time." She said.

Benjamin looked at her and replied. "Not with you smiling and acting like that, it isn't."

"I think I'm ready, for real."

Stacy added. "Trust me, when that baby is ready to come out, you will not be acting like you're acting. You'll hardly be able to walk, talk or breathe."

"I know I'm not in a lot of pain, but I really do think it's time." She walked over to the phone and called her mom's home in Mississippi, collect.

"Hello." It was her brother, Eugene.

"Gene? This is Evette."

"What's going on, girl?" You could hear the smile in his voice.

"Nothing much. I just called to let mommy know that she's going to have a little grandson or daughter some time today."

"What? Are you sure? You don't sound like someone who is about to give birth."

"I know I don't, but I am. I'll call her from the hospital when the baby is born. I love you. Talk to you later."

"I love you, too. Take care."

Stacy picked up the phone and called out from work so she could be with her, but Benjamin went in. He felt it was a false alarm. Evette frowned. She felt a sharp pain.

"I think you need to go lay down." Stacy suggested. Evette headed for the stairs.

"No! No! The last thing you need to do is climb those steps. You can lie down in our room."

She obeyed.

They tried to contact her physician and after about ½ an hour, they learned that he'd gone on vacation. His associate was going to have to deliver her baby.

"This is Doctor Grace. Is this Mrs. Worthington?"

"Yes."

"How are you feeling?"

"Fine."

"Have you started timing your contractions?"

"Yes." She laid there on her right side rocking back and forth, rubbing her stomach with her left hand. Alexander tried to massage her lower back. "They are about 15 minutes apart."

"You don't sound like you're in a lot of pain. Is this your first baby?"

"Yes, it is and no I'm not experiencing a lot of pain."

"Mrs. Worthington, did you exercise a lot while you were pregnant?"

"I wasn't supposed to, but yes, I did."

"Come to the hospital. Now!" And she hung up. Evette's mouth dropped open.

"What did she say?" Asked Stacy.

"She asked me if this was my first baby and if I'd done a lot of exercising while I was pregnant. I said yes, and she said to come to the hospital now."

They all headed out the door and climbed into the mini van. Benjamin had taken the Impala to work. It took forever, seemingly, to get there because they had to drop Stacy's children off at the church for Sunday school. That trip took about 45 minutes.

When they arrived at the church, the three girls hopped out and ran in screaming, "Aunt Evette is having the baby! Aunt Evette is having the baby!"

Edith ran out to the van and slid the side door open. Evette was holding her stomach and breathing the way she'd always heard that you're supposed to breathe when in labor. By this time, she was starting to hurt, not badly, but enough to make her groan.

"Are you sure it's not a false alarm? You're not acting like it's the real thing." Evette just looked at her and then rested her head on Alexander's shoulders. Edith reached over and pressed her hand down hard on Evette's stomach making her yell out. Evette was pissed off. *Now, she sees me in pain and she's going to push me in the stomach?* What Evette didn't know is that contractions can be felt that way and her mother-in-law was just trying to see if her labor was real.

Edith lifted her hand. "Get her to the hospital, quick!" She slammed the door and they pulled off.

It took almost an hour to get to GBMC Hospital, but when they arrived, she was immediately placed in a wheel chair and taken in. Stacy assisted Alexander with the paper work while they laid Evette on a table and placed a belt around her waist to monitor her contractions. They checked her and she had dilated some more.

"So, Mrs. Worthington, how are you feeling?"

"All things considered, I'm fine." She grimaced in pain.

"Well," the nurse said as she slid the glove off her hand, "it appears that you're six centimeters." She looked at the attendants. "Take her to LDR number four and get her prepped." They began to push her down the hall.

One of the escorts began asking questions. "Have you eaten anything in the past twelve hours?"

"No."

"Have you had anything to drink within the past three hours?"

"No."

"Is there a possibility that you could have HIV, herpes, gonorrhea, or any other disease that could be transferred to the child?"

"No. No. No. And No."

"I'm sorry Mrs. Worthington but we have to ask for the sake of the baby's safety."

Another contraction hit her as they were sliding her from the gurney to the bed.

"Mrs. Worthington, please don't jump. We don't want to risk dropping you."

They placed her in the bed and strapped a monitor around her waist.

"Don't worry; nature will take its course. All we do is watch the process as it takes place and make sure that you both come through alright." They exited the room.

It was beautiful. The room had the look and feel of a real bedroom. It was filled with furniture, mirrors, a television, beautiful curtains and wall décor. What caught Evette's attention the most was the clock that hung on the wall to her left. It was 11:05a.m. She thought within herself, *I'm going to have this baby by 12noon.* She was petrified. Other sisters had told her a lot of 'labor room horror stories' and she expected to be in hard labor for at least 12 hours. She really hoped that God would grant her what she was praying for.

Stacy sat in the corner in a recliner to her right rocking back and forth. Alexander stood by her bedside holding her right hand in his right hand while he wiped her forehead with his left.

"Will you please stop that? It's irritating." She pushed his hand away from her head.

"I'm sorry, baby. I'm just trying to help you."

Stacy sat up and looked at the monitor. "She's about to start hating you right about now, Alexander."

A pain hit her in her lower back, worked its way around her stomach and rested there. She saw her muscles tighten and rise like an egg about to hatch. She bore down, held her breath and when it heightened she moaned.

The nurse checked her and she was seven centimeters. "Mrs. Worthington, do you think you'll want something for pain?"

"Yes."

"No!" Evette and the nurse were startled. Alexander didn't want her to have anything to relieve her of the pain. It wasn't because he wanted to see her suffer, they had discussed this before they got married and had agreed that she wouldn't take anything. He forgot that when people are in pain, things change.

"Excuse me?" The nurse said. "Did you just say that you don't want your wife to have anything for her pain?"

"That's correct." He looked down at Evette. "Baby, I don't think you need it."

The nurse's mouth dropped.

Evette responded. "I don't think I can do this, Alexander."

"Baby, the Lord is able to see you through."

"No, He isn't. I want something."

Stacy laughed.

The nurse exited the room to get the anesthesiologist. He was tall, well built and looked like he was in his mid-thirties. He began to talk to her about the possible side effects of the epidural.

"You may experience lower back pain…"

Alexander interrupted. "See baby. You already have back problems. You don't want to add to that."

"Some women have been known to experience moments of temporary paralysis from the waist down." The doctor continued.

"See that? You could be paralyzed."

Stacy jumped in. "It's against our religion to have stuff for pain."

Evette looked at her. "Where did you get that from? That's not in the Bible."

The nurse became frustrated.

"Excuse me, Mr. Worthington," She looked at Stacy. "Ma'am. I don't mean to be rude, but you two are not the ones in pain here. She is." She shot a look at Evette. "Now, do you want something for pain?"

"Yes." At that moment she had a contraction and screamed "Jesus!" The nurse checked her and she was eight centimeters.

"Well, if you want something, now is the time to get it."

"Yes, please! Yes!" But by the time the doctor went to wash his hands, almost immediately, another contraction hit. She had jumped from eight to ten centimeters just that quickly and the baby was coming out.

"Oh, God! Oh, God!" She yelled, but it was too late. He or she was coming out and fast.

Alexander thought within himself, *Lord, thank you for answering my prayer.* Evette shot a look at him because in her heart, she knew that he'd prayed and asked God to speed things along so she wouldn't have to have the epidural. She had not had Lamaze classes, so she didn't know how to push. She ended up straining so hard, she hurt her chest.

"No, no, Mrs. Worthington. Push as though you're having a bowel movement."

"I can't." She started to cry.

"Yes, you can and you will. You're a strong woman and you can do this."

Evette shook her head as tears began streaming down her cheeks. She completely turned away from Alexander.

"Mrs. Worthington." The nurse said. "I want you to listen to me. I want you to blow and pant like a dog between the pains." She began to do it and Evette mimicked her. Another contraction began and she began to push.

"Come on. That's it. Push! Push! You're doing great. Okay, that's it. Now, relax with it. Now that that one is over, let's breathe through until the next one."

Evette looked at the clock. It was 11:40a.m. She thought, *God please. By 12noon* and another one came.

"Don't panic. Just push. That's it, Mrs. Worthington."

The doctor spoke up. "I see the head. Boy, this kid has a lot of hair. Did you have a lot of heart burn?"

"Yes." She grunted.

"Now, Mrs. Worthington," the doctor added, "This is going to sound crazy, but I really need you to stop pushing."

"What?"

"That's right. I need to clear the baby's air ways."

It only took a minute or two, but it felt like forever. All Evette wanted to do was get this baby out of her. Every part of her body wanted to push, but she followed the doctor's orders. Then another pain hit.

"Okay. You can start pushing again." The nurse began to encourage her again.

"Come on. Give it everything you've got." She glanced over at Alexander. "Mr. Worthington, can you grab her right leg and lift it up while I grab the left one, please?" He did.

"What are you doing to me?" She blurted. "Horses are treated with more dignity."

"This will help to speed things along. Raise up and push." She did, with all she had. She felt the baby as it plopped out of her, and she heard the cry of the child's voice.

"Congratulations, Mr. and Mrs. Worthington. You have a son."

Evette began to laugh. They'd been praying for a son and God had granted their request. The nurse smiled and said "Mrs. Worthington, this is the best 'first delivery' I've ever seen. It's almost as if you were made to have babies."

"I don't know about that." Evette replied, and smiled.

Alexander hugged and kissed her. "Baby, you did it. You did it."

The doctor let him cut the umbilical cord. Then they wiped him off, wrapped him up and handed him to his daddy. Alexander began to sing worship songs to him as he rocked this special part of himself in his arms.

Okay, Mr. Worthington, we need to get your little man all cleaned up." The nurse took the baby and Alexander picked up the phone and called the church.

"Hello. Mom? This is Alexander. I just wanted to let you know that we had the baby."

What does he mean by 'we?' I'm the one that went trough this. All he did was watch.

"I don't know how much he weighs or how long he is. He just came out. Yes, ma'am. It's a boy. Okay. Okay. Okay. I'll see you in a little bit." He hung up the phone and watched as they extracted and checked the after birth. They finished cleaning Evette up and left them to be alone.

Stacy sat quietly in the corner. She was upset that after all these years of trying to have the first grandson that would bare the Worthington name, Evette was the one God blessed with the honor. There was only one thing that they both had in common. They both wanted to be accepted by the Worthington family but neither of them was.

They didn't want Evette and Stacy to become close because they were afraid she would tell Evette that Benjamin was beating her. However, she already knew. She'd watched Stacy long enough to see the signs; withdrawn in Benjamin's presence or at times, trying much too hard to please him; moody and abrasive with the children; depressed most of the time; always wearing sunglasses and scarves. She'd seen enough abused women at the church in Mississippi to know what was going on.

The family blamed Stacy for what Benjamin had become; a backslidden, wife beating, drug addict. It's amazing how people never blame themselves for their problems until they've run out of other people to blame.

They moved Evette into a regular room. Only one sister form the church called to see how she was doing. It was Sister Leigh.

"Praise the Lord, Evangelist Worthington."

"Sister Leigh, is that you?"

"Yeah. Congratulations on your little blessing. I don't think I have to ask what you named him." She laughed. She was genuinely happy for her.

"Girl, you know Minister Worthington lay claims on that the moment we found out I was pregnant."

"Is he a jr.?"

"No. His name is Alexander Antonio Worthington, II. He's 21 inches long and he weighed 8lbs, 11ozs."

"Who does he look like?"

"Believe it or not, he looks like a combination of both of us."

"Well, I'm not going to hold you. I just wanted to call and see how you all were doing. I love you, Sis and I'm praying for you."

"I love you, too. God bless you."

As she was hanging up the phone, the nurse came in with little A.J.

"Somebody wants to see you," she said as she handed her son to her.

"Thank you."

"I think I'll leave you two alone."

She left and gently closed the door behind her. Evette sat on the edge of the bed staring down at her very own miracle baby and she smiled. Tears gently caressed her cheeks as she began to count all of his fingers and toes. She lifted her eyes toward Heaven and began to worship God.

"Lord, I thank you. It wasn't even as bad as I'd thought it would be." Then she looked back at A.J. and thought *how can something this big come out of me?*

Stacy, Alexander, Elder and Evangelist Worthington entered the room.

"Let me hold my grandson." Edith said as she reached for the baby. *She didn't even ask me how I'm doing.* Evette handed him to her. "Oh, look at him Elder Worthington."

I wonder why she always addresses him like that? He's her husband for crying out loud. Doesn't she know its okay to call him baby or dear?

"He looks just like me and your mother."

"I think he looks like your son and I." Evette said.

"No. No. He has your mother's strong forehead and my nose. See?"

"Whatever."

"Well, we're going to go and let you get some well deserved rest."

Alexander wanted to spend the night but he had to go to work the next day. They all gave her a hug and he held his son one more time and said good night. She was left alone with God and her son. Eight days later, they moved into their own apartment.

It was with the help of Benjamin's wife that they were able to get the apartment. She just so happened to know the lady that was the manager and she was also willing to co-sign for them. It was three days before Thanksgiving and because Alexander worked during the daytime, Evette ended up doing the bulk of the unpacking alone. She wanted to have everything in order for the holidays. No one in his family came to help her, despite the fact that they lived up the street - walking distance. The day before Thanksgiving, he came home and she'd finished everything. As usual, his bath water was in the tub nice and hot, just the way he liked it. The table was set and they all sat down for a nice dinner.

"Baby, the place looks great."

"Thank you."

"I'm sure it took a lot out of you. Are you alright?"

"Yeah, I guess I am."

"What's that supposed to mean?" He bit into another mouthful of meat loaf and potatoes.

"Well, I think I over did things by moving those heavy boxes."

"My mother used to do that kinda stuff and a lot more after she'd given birth."

No he didn't just compare me with his momma! She chuckled to keep from going off. "Baby, I'm not your mother."

Seeing that he had just stuck his foot in his mouth, he quickly replied, "No, you're not my mother. She's not half as fine as you."

"Or half as good of a cook as me either."

"Or half as good of a cook as you either."

He leaned across the table and kissed her on the nape of her neck.

"Are you ready to study the Sunday school lesson for this week?" He asked

"I'm a step ahead of you." She pointed to the living room table. He looked over her shoulders and saw the books and their Bibles spread across it.

"That's why I love you so much." He smiled.

"Oh, yeah? I thought you loved me because I'm a freak in the bedroom."

"I never knew you as a 'freak' until after we said 'I do.' Before then, though, I did know you as being thoughtful and considerate."

"Why, Mr. Worthington, I do declare." She said, in her best southern voice as she put her right hand across her chest and blushed. "I think you're in for a wild night tonight, sir."

After they finished studying, Evette put their son to bed. Alexander helped her to wash her hair while they both showered together. They enjoyed taking turns washing each other's bodies. As the water rinsed the soap away, they began to gently kiss. His hands caressed the curves of her body as he lowered his head to suck the milk that was left in her breasts from nursing the baby. She threw her head back and groaned as his lips sweetly massaged their way down further and further to the center of her passions and right before his tongue reached her clitoris, he stopped.

She didn't say anything, because she knew he'd never experienced that level of sexual pleasure before, but in her heart, she was greatly disappointed. She knew that she would have to increase the pace of their sexual relationship because aside from masturbation, oral sex had been the only means by which she was ever able to climax. She felt that having sex without having an orgasm was like eating and not getting full. After a while, you just get tired of chewing and you walk away from the table.

So, she lifted his head and began to kiss his chest. Despite the fact that she was the only woman he'd ever been with, she never tried to short-change him sexually. She treated him as if he was a man who'd been with countless amounts of women. In short, he was stone cold whipped! After she finished licking and sucking his chest. She began to move downward. He almost collapsed with pleasure, so she quickly turned the shower off, grabbed a towel to half dry themselves and quickly proceeded to the bedroom.

Once there, she picked up where she left off, but this time she didn't stop. She kept going until she reached his penis and she gave an award winning performance. She didn't allow him to climax, though, because she wanted him to be inside of her when he came. She liked the way his penis felt as it throbbed inside her vagina during his climaxes. She had so many tricks up her sleeve, but it was still too early in the marriage to let all of them out of the box. She wanted to have some things left for him to enjoy as time went on. She didn't want the sexual aspect of their relationship to grow old, tired and stale.

The next night, much to her dismay, Alexander left her and his son home alone so that he could spend Thanksgiving with his family. She was beyond hurt and she cried for hours. The worst part was that when he finally did come home, around 11:30 p.m., he hadn't even thought to bring her something to eat. He had to leave, go back to his mom's house to get them to fix her a plate and then return. When she took the aluminum foil off of it, she handed it back to him. It looked as if it had been thrown together. She lost her appetite at the very sight of it.

"Alexander, how could you be so inconsiderate?"

"Baby, what are you talking about?"

"I was home worried about you. You couldn't call me and let me know what was going on? You said that you would be right back and when you didn't show up, I was thinking that you all had been in an accident or something."

"Mom took us to the house for Thanksgiving dinner. I didn't think you would mind, since you can't go out of the house right now anyway."

"Just forget it. You don't understand."

"What don't I understand?"

"You don't understand that I worry about you when I don't hear from you. You don't understand that I need you to call me. Not because I'm trying to keep tabs on you, but so that I can know that you're okay. What if something had happened to you?"

"But it didn't."

"I know, but what if something did? How would I know?" She threw up her hands. "Just forget about it. I'm going to bed."

"Baby, I'm sorry. I just wanted to spend some time with my family."

As she walked into the bedroom, she glanced back at him and said, "I thought A.J. and I were your family."

The Assignment

"I've been observing your lifestyle." Elder Bogess told her. "And I want to give you more freedom in ministry. The women need someone around their age group that can relate to them. I want you to get close to the ones I point out to you, but you can't let them know that I'm sending you to them. They have to feel they can trust you."

Evette sat and listened. She was elated that doors in ministry were opening up for her, even if they were politically based ones. He continued.

"There is one exception, though. You cannot take anyone's confessions. If they've sinned and need to confess, encourage them to repent but direct them to speak to me. Is that clear?"

"Yes, sir. Very."

"Good. Your first assignment is Sister Baker."

"What's her issue?"

"She's been very depressed. She's been pregnant since she's been saved."

"That's enough to do it."

"What was that?"

"Oh, nothing. You were saying?"

"She won't open up to me. So, I need you to get close to her. Find out what's going on in her head and report it back to me. Understood?"

"Understood." She stood to leave. He extended his hand to shake hers and smiled.

"Sister Worthington, if you continue to be submissive and obedient, the Lord will bless you to go far in ministry." He nodded. "Very far indeed." She left.

She saw her sitting in the back of the church with her two children. Her husband was in the dining hall with some of the other brothers laughing and talking.

"Praise the Lord, Sis Baker. How are you doing today?"

"Fine." She snapped.

Evette thought, *this is going to be a little more challenging than I thought.* Since her youngest son was three weeks younger that A.J., she used them as icebreakers.

"How is little Ahkiem doing? He's growing nicely. I think we're going to have to pray for God to save him at a very early age."

She looked puzzled. "Why is that?"

"Because as cute as he is, little girls are going to be chasing him down, calling your house and getting on your nerves."

She laughed. "Evangelist Worthington, you're so crazy."

I knew that would get her. That one always gets 'em. "I'm serious, girl. Anyway, I wanted to know if you and your husband would like to join us for dinner. Our treat."

"Sure. When?"

"Now."

"Well, I'll have to check with Brother Baker first and see if he says it's okay."

"I'll go with you." Evette said and winked at her. "Sometimes men say 'yes' a little easier when someone else is standing there listening."

Sure enough, he felt as if he'd been put on the spot and had no choice but to say yes. It's amazing how some men can be filled with so much pride until they'd rather see their family be hungry than to humble themselves and be blessed. Thank God, Brother Baker was in a less prideful mood.

Since neither couple had much money, they went to Denny's. It was over an hour and a half before someone took their order and another hour before their food was served. No one seemed to mind, but Evette was fuming.

They had been seated near the restrooms despite the fact that there were plenty of good seats available and every white person that had come in after them had been served before them. Evette wanted to call a lawyer and in the months that followed, Alexander wished he had allowed her to because Denny's went through a major lawsuit for discriminating against its African American customers. His mom had taught them that it was wrong to take people to court, so once again his upbringing caused them to seemingly miss out.

Dinner was cold and they had to send it back but despite the poor service, they enjoyed one another's company. They talked about their children, their childhoods, their dreams, and ministry. They didn't talk much about the future. Later, Evette found out why. Sister Glenda didn't feel she had much of a future to look forward to.

Mentoring

"Evangelist Worthington, may I ask you a favor?"

"Sure. Anything." She answered.

"Would you be my mentor, my spiritual big sister?"

I don't know the first thing about mentoring a grown woman. I've never had anyone to take me under their wings so how could I take a grown woman under mine?

"Sure. I'd be glad to." *What am I getting myself into?* "We can start tomorrow."

"Wonderful!" She was so excited. They were both housewives at the time, so it was easy to meet at noon, daily.

"I'll be at your house around 12 noon. We'll start with a study of the book of Acts."

They embraced one another, Evette not knowing that she'd later regret the moment she ever accepted this assignment.

In the months that followed, Evette literally became everything to Glenda that she'd never had for herself, a mentor, a big sister, a spiritual advisor, and a confidante. She even taught her how to pray and cry out to God without being intimidated by the presence of others.

Soon, Elder Bogess became concerned about the turn their relationship was taking. Glenda was no longer quiet and depressed. She became outgoing and expressive of her thoughts and opinions. Some leaders want the female members of their congregations to be free but in a quiet kind of way. They forget that knowledge brings boldness. It also cuts against the grain of traditionalism, because when people embrace truth they quickly let go of everything else that's false.

"Sister Worthington, may I ask you a few doctrinal questions?"

"You can ask me anything you like."

"Is it a sin to wear make-up and jewelry or to use birth control?"

Evette almost choked on her salad. *Oh, God, no she didn't go there. Should I tell her the truth and risk my*

position in the church or should I continue in the doctrinal
traditions of the organization? God, help me find the words.
She cleared her throat.

"Well, do you want a lie or do you want the truth?"

"Sister Evette, I want the truth. Every time I've ever
asked someone in this church, they never answer the
question but instead make me feel like something is wrong
with me for asking."

"Well, I can only tell you what the Bible says, or
rather what it does not say. There is absolutely no scripture
in the Bible that says wearing make-up, jewelry or pants is
a sin for women. As far as birth control goes, the Bible
doesn't say anything for it or against it. So, I think that it's
an area that each couple should pray about. Yes, the Bible
says that 'children are the heritage of the Lord' and that
we'd be happy if our quiver is full of them, but it doesn't
say how many we should have."

"Well, what about Jacob and Abraham and the other
men who had so many children? And what about Onan
whom God killed for withdrawing from his wife?"

"What about keeping the word in its proper context?"
Evette stated.

"What does that mean?"

"Keep it in context. Abraham had only one child by
Sarah. The rest were by his second Ethiopian wife. Jacob,
if you recall, had children by four different women who, by
the way, were in competition with each other to see who
could have the most children. As far as Onan goes, God
killed him because he broke the Law, not because he used
the withdrawal method. Furthermore, all of those men
were, by today's standards, multi-millionaires, so they
could afford to not only have children by their wives and
concubines, but they also had enough money to provide for
quite a few servants and their families as well."

"He broke the Law?"

"Yes, and breaking the Law was punishable by
death."

"What law? I don't understand."

"The Law stated that if any man married a woman and died without having had children by her, his next oldest brother was supposed to marry her and have children. Here's the catch. The Bible says that the children would be considered the seed of the *dead* brother. That's why Onan spilled his seed on the ground. He knew that the children would not be considered his and that's why God killed him. His motive for withdrawing was wrong."

"So, why do they teach us this stuff?"

"Because it's easier for women to fill the pews by giving birth than it is for them to do like Jesus said and go out into the highways and byways and compel men to come. "Also," she added, "I think how we were breeded during slavery has something to do with it."

"Thank you so much. I had resigned myself to the thought of being pregnant every year and not being able to return to college until I was in my forties, like Sister Worthington, your mother-in-law. Thanks for helping me."

After that conversation, Sister Glenda began wearing small, gold earrings and she started taking birth control pills. She also talked her father into babysitting the kids while she returned to college to finish her degree. She asked her father because her mother was dead.

A Hard Lesson in Politics

He approached her where she sat. "Sister Worthington, may I have a talk with you?" He said, sternly.

Why is he calling me Sister Worthington? I must be in trouble, but I haven't done anything.

"Yes, sir."

"I asked you to go to these sisters and be a mentor to them."

"And I did."

"I asked you to get close to them. To find out what was going on inside of them."

"And I did."

"I asked you to encourage them and to help them." His voice began to rise.

"Yes, sir, and I did. I did everything you asked me to do."

He slammed his fist on the table. "But I did NOT tell you to tell them things contrary to the teachings of this ministry! Sister Baker is wearing earrings and is on birth control. Sister Axel heard and now she's wearing make-up and bracelets...."

She interrupted. "They're only small ones, and neither of them can afford to have any more children."

"That is not your call!"

"But all I did was telling them the truth. Most of the stuff that we tell people will put them in Hell isn't even found in the Bible. You know that."

"That does not give you the right to go against the traditions of this organization! The *Apostolic Churches of Pentecost* and its traditions were here before you were born and when you die, it will still be going strong."

"But Elder Bogess..."

"Don't 'but' me, young lady. You're silenced!"

"But Elder Bogess!"

"You heard me."

"Silenced for what?"

"Rebellion! The Bible says that rebellion is as the sin of witchcraft. I don't want you doing anything in this church for the next 90 days."

" Ninety days? But that's not right. All I did was tell them the truth."

"That is not the 'truth' that we teach. You can't preach here or anywhere else. I'll inform your mother-in-law to assign your Sunday school class to someone else for this quarter. You cannot testify, you cannot direct the choir and I am relieving you of all duties for the Missionary Department for 90 days." He got up and walked away.

She sat there and began to cry. This was her first lesson in church politics. At that moment, she wished she'd never agreed to this 'assignment.' She thought, *maybe it's better to leave people in doctrinal bondage than to free them and risk being hurt yourself. No, that's not right. The Bible says that we should know the truth and it will make us free. It is better to obey God than man, even if man seems to be running the church his way instead of God's.*

It was the longest season of her life. In times past, days seemed to fly by, but now that she was silenced, it felt as though time had been as well. The pastor gave no reason to the church or its leaders, so they were all left to allow their minds to wander and as people often do, they thought of the absolute worst.

"I wonder what Sister Worthington did?" Asked Sister Axel.

"It must be pretty bad because she can't even praise the Lord during the services." Responded Sister Baker.

"You think it was adultery?"

"You know it had to be. Why else would the Pastor have come down so hard on her?"

"All this time, she's going around calling herself trying to help us and she needed help herself."

"I know, girl. She actually taught me how to pray. She obviously wasn't praying herself."

"So, are you going to stop wearing earrings and stop taking birth control pills? She taught you about that, too, you know."

"Girl, no! Truth is truth, even if it does come from the mouth of a hypocrite."

They walked off. Evette got up and went downstairs to the restroom and cried. They knew she was sitting no more than five feet away from them and they made every effort to speak as loud as possible to ensure that she heard them.

She wiped the tears from her eyes. She looked at her reflection and thought *it's amazing that the people Jesus said would be known for their love are some of the meanest heffas you'd ever come across. And to think I invested so much of my time and myself into them. How soon, how soon, they turn.*

When the 90 days were ended, Evette wasn't the same. Her rapport with the female members of the congregation wasn't the same either. Slowly, she became the expressed image of what the other women once were. What she had worked so hard to help them change from, is the very person she became. She became quiet, withdrawn, and depressed. Whereas she once looked forward to church, she now began to loathe being there. The very thought of being in church sent her into deep states of depression, that sometimes lasted for weeks. She also began to sit in the very back of the church in somewhat of a catatonic state.

One day, Mother Bailey approached her.

"You know, they always told me that when folks start sitting in the back of the church, it won't be too long before they are gone out of the church."

Evette didn't respond. She didn't even lift an eyebrow.

"Where is the passion you used to have, child? Whatever happened to the woman that stood behind that podium up there and preached from the depths of her soul? Your passion for God is what keeps you going. Now baby, when we don't direct our passions toward the things of God, the Devil will find another direction for our passions. Don't let your passion fall." She gave her a hug and walked away.

It was too late. Her passion for the things of God had already fallen. When it comes to religious politics, you either play the game or leave the stadium. There's no room, seemingly, for those who are too honest. The whole evangelistic scene had turned into something Jesus would undoubtedly puke at. Back in the day, they used to call it 'harvesting the fields of the Lord.' Now, they were calling it 'working the circuit.' For most, it was no longer about saving souls. It was no longer about the work of the Lord. It was about building your own dynasty, about making a profit and getting 'what's due' to you.

Most people can't tell when they are about to be had, because sometimes it's covered up, by 'I hear the Lord saying' or some other phrase like that. Then they'd ask for so many people to give $100 and gradually decrease to $50, then $25, $10 and so on. They would ask people to line up down the center isle in a straight line to put their money in the basket and be prayed over. What they were really doing was counting heads as the people walk by so when they went in the back to count the money, the preacher already had a general idea of how much was collected. This way, you couldn't 'cheat them' out of what was due them. Or, if they try to demand more money, you couldn't lie to them and say that there was not enough because they already knew what was collected.

Evette always respected those who were honest enough to let the people know that the budget had not been met and then inform the people of how much more was needed. *Church folk can be so ignorant and vulnerable. We trust too much and as a result, we get fleeced.* Evette thought.

There was a time when people were just glad to have the opportunity to be used by God. Now, from what Evette saw, if you had a small church they wouldn't come to preach or teach there; not enough people for them to get a good offering. If they did come, you had to send them so much money up front, provide first class round trip airfare, first rate lodging accommodations, dry clean their clothes, pay for their meals, provide servants (adjutants) and escorts for them and then give them half of all the offerings you collected while they were there.

On the other hand, one could easily understand how it got this way. If the saints had done right at a lesser level, it wouldn't have escalated to the racket that she felt it had become.

The best thing about being silenced in the church is that by not being able to talk, you're able to do more listening. Evette heard other ministers and Evangelists speak of their experiences.

"Man, I cannot believe that Pastor!"

"What did he do?"

"What did he do? Man, he heard me preach at *True Faith* and invited me to speak at his church. Mind you, his church is in Texas."

"What's the big deal about that?"

"I'll tell you what the big deal is. I'm here in Baltimore; his church is in San Antonio, Texas. He told me that they couldn't afford to send for me, so I took off work, drove all the way down there and preached a five day revival."

"Again, I ask, what's so wrong with that?"

"Just listen. Every night the Pastor took two offerings from the people - one for the church and one for me. At the end of the week, I had sweated out all of my clothes, had no money to clean them and was physically drained. Not only was I preaching every night, but every day people in his congregation were coming to me for counseling."

He continued. "Friday night's service ended a little after midnight, because he wanted me to individually pray for every member. Before I left, they handed me an envelope and I drove off. On the way back to Baltimore, I stopped for gas, opened the envelope and guess what it was filled with?"

"What?"

"Food stamps!"

Evette remembered thinking *how could they have lied and played him like that? Those people thought their money was going to the Evangelist and the Pastor kept it.* Then she recalled a conversation that had occurred during a deacon's meeting. One of the Deacons at St. Andrews openly admitted that when the church invites speakers, if the speaker's offering is more than the church's offering, he'd give the speaker the lesser amount. *Crooks breeding crooks,* she thought and she vowed that she would never prostitute her gifts or fleece and pimp the people of God.

As the ninety days ended, she noticed that A.J. was growing well. He was so cute and loved to have his picture taken. Alexander loved his son, though he didn't spend time with him during church. That was a woman's job. He sat in the pulpit and left Evette to tend to him. Even when she started preaching again, Alexander expected her to leave the pulpit when she was finished to relieve him of his son.

Evette gradually lost sight of God. She began to focus on the things that pleased the people. She was caught in the cycle of religious politics and her passion for God had fallen. She'd forgotten the promise she'd made to herself and now it was no longer about God, it was about the game.

Her marriage was shot to Hell. After the assault, every time Alexander would touch her, she'd have flashbacks. There were times that she could smell Marvin's body odor in the apartment and would check the closets and under the beds to make sure he wasn't there. As a result of Alexander not being there for her emotionally, she began to despise him. She no longer felt as if she was his wife. She felt like a roommate. Once, she'd told him that she felt as if they were just roommates that slept together occasionally. After a while her sex drive dwindled. She no longer desired him. It's hard for a woman to desire a man when she no longer respects him and feels that he doesn't love her. Tried as she did, all of her passion was gone.

She sat her mind toward moving up within the political ranks of the church and it was working. She not only got her old responsibilities back within the Missionary Department, she was voted Vice President. She'd preached her first three-day revival, had been asked to be one of the guest speakers at a street service, and was receiving phone calls from other churches to minister to their congregations. At one of the Organization's conferences, she'd been asked to speak. She was just sitting in the audience and at the last minute she was called upon to preach. She was only given 15 minutes, but by the time she sat down, everyone was on their feet praising God. Even Bishop Langley complimented her and a good word from him meant a lot to someone's ministerial career.

When word of what happened got around, a lot of the males in ministry became upset because they'd been preaching longer and had yet to be asked to speak in one of the conferences. They began to treat her with much disdain. One even went as far as to point to A.J., her son, and say that having babies was her ministry. She let him know that his statement was the most sexist thing she'd ever heard in her life and that she would appreciate him not having anything to do with Alexander, lest that 'demon' transfers from him to her husband. Of course, he got pissed and stormed off to start a rumor that she was a feminist. This was to be her second painful lesson. When it comes to church politics, it's a man's world. For a woman to exceed the ranks she has to be almost 10 times more anointed than a man and even then she's given a hard time.

I wonder if the women in the national arena went through this sexist, political crap before they ascended to where they are now? She thought, as she felt herself being pulled faster into this ever-increasing downward spin.

The Fall

The blizzard of 1996 was one that would never be forgotten. They went to bed that Saturday night thinking that they would be able to go grocery shopping after church and when they woke up Sunday morning there was at least two feet of snow on the ground. The refrigerator was empty, so Alexander called to his mom's house and asked if they could come over there until the storm and the streets became bearable. His oldest brother met them at their apartment so that he could assist with the bags and with A.J. By the time they got half way up the street, a white man in a S.U.V. pulled up beside them and offered a ride. Of course, they were grateful.

Once they were safe and sound inside, Evette proceeded to assist Alexander's mom with dinner. The house was unbelievably full to capacity. Including the children, there were nineteen in all. Alexander, Evette and A.J. slept wherever they could find space. The next night, as always, she went upstairs to one of the younger brother's rooms to watch television.

After the assault and attempted rape in the beginning of their marriage, things began to go downhill between her and Alexander and she found herself leaning on John more and more. Whereas Alexander never wanted to even mention what had happened, John allowed her to vent and cry on his shoulders. He was always her friend before, but now he began to walk in the posture that her husband should have had. He became her protector, her sounding board, her encouragement, and her strength.

During the first season of their homeless state when they lived in his sister's attic, Evette would have to walk up the street to the house to prepare Alexander's dinner because the kitchen in the house wasn't up to par. John was like a lion guarding its cub when it came to Evette. If she needed to use the bathroom, he would go in first, check to ensure that the brother who'd tried to rape her wasn't in there and then he would stand outside the door to further ensure her safety. As the months passed, they grew closer and closer.

That night, he escorted her upstairs to his room in the attic and they sat on the bed watching a sitcom that featured a new vocal artist named Brandy. The show was entitled *Moesha*. They began to talk about their fears.

"Evette, what's your greatest fear?" He asked.

"Other than going to Hell? Committing adultery." She responded. "And yours?"

"Not being able to have children." He said.

The conversation continued and after a while he began to tell her that he'd been having dreams about her. He told her that he'd been dreaming about making love to her and how lately he'd found himself watching the nipples of her breasts in church. He asked if she'd ever looked at him in that way and she was honest. She told him that once, while they were talking outside the house, the thought had crossed her mind of how soft his lips seemed, but she quickly dismissed it.

He asked her to kiss him and she said no. He asked why and she told him 'if anything were to ever happen between us, you would lie and say that I seduced you.'

"Do you believe that I'll kiss you?" He asked

"No, I don't." Evette said.

At that moment, he leaned over and kissed her. His lips were softer than she had imagined them to be and even though she never really liked kissing anyone other than Love, she found herself swimming in him. She wanted so badly to be held by someone that she felt cared about her, someone she could trust to be there for her. Besides, she owed him that much, or so she thought at the time. What was actually going on was a merger of the lines between reality and insanity that began that Monday morning, in 1993, when she was attacked.

After that night, they were together three times. The last time, they went all the way. Each time something happened, she would tell Alexander. John felt as though she was trying to get back at Alexander for not being there for her and for going along with the family's wishes to squash what happened. Evette denied it, of course, but years later, she realized that subconsciously, that's exactly what she had done.

She'd never been the type to try to make excuses for her actions and she never tried to blame anyone for any of the decisions that she made. That was certainly a bad decision and when it was over, her hallucinations increased tremendously. She still continued to teach Bible class, and preach even though she knew that once she confessed that would all be over.

Two months after she'd weaned A.J., she found out she was six weeks pregnant. A lot of the men rejoiced because the Organization didn't believe that women should function in ministry while pregnant. Elder Allen came to her again. He was about 6'9" and overweight. He always wore black suits and had several teeth missing in the front of his mouth. There is something about Baltimore men, young or old; they don't seem to take care of their teeth.

"I see you're busy fulfilling your rightful ministry."

She walked away without responding. Some people aren't worth the effort it takes to even think of a good comeback.

One evening, she began spotting blood. She called her primary care physician and he told her that if the bleeding continued by the next morning, to come to the emergency room at GBMC. She did. By now, she was entering the second trimester. She lay on the table for hours in pain. Alexander couldn't find anyone to keep A.J. so he had to bring him to the hospital. He stood there clutching his son and watching his wife as she bled on the table. The baby hadn't come out yet and she was losing a lot of blood. Every time she had a contraction, blood and blood clots gushed from her and the nurses would collect it.

After two hours of her lying there bleeding and contracting, they finally rushed her to an operating room to perform an emergency DNC.

"How are you feeling, sweetie?" Asked the nurse as she rubbed her forehead.

"I have to use the bathroom." Evette said.

"You can use it right here on the table."

In shock, she responded. "Are you crazy? I can't use the bathroom on the table, that's nasty."

Those were the last words she remembered saying. Hours later, she woke up in Recovery and Alexander and A.J. were right there holding her hands.

"Baby, how are you feeling?" Alexander asked.

"Sluggish, but fine." She said, in a semi state of consciousness.

The Anesthesiologist looked at her. "Oh, so you're awake now? Well, I want to give you at least two more hours before we let you go. I want to make sure the anesthesia has worn off a bit more."

"What time is it?" Evette asked as she looked around the room for a clock.

The doctor answered. "You've been in here for about six hours if that's what you want to know. Just give us two more and you can be on your way." She walked over and patted Evette's hand. "You'll be okay just don't try having any more kids for a while. Give your body a chance to heal. Okay?"

"Okay."

Two hours later, they were on their way. She thought they'd be going home, but Alexander took her to his mother's house instead. *No he isn't bringing me here,* she thought.

They already knew that she'd lost the babies. She knew she was pregnant with twins but she wanted it to be a surprise. It had been over thirty years since the last multiple birth in Alexander's family and she thought that God had finally given her the honor of being the one to break the mold, but because of a violent act that she told herself God allowed, her babies were now dead. She blamed God because she was always taught that nothing happens to you except He permits it to. Slowly, she sank deeper and deeper into a state of emotional isolation. To make matters worse, the family felt it was her fault for being so proud.

"The only reason God would allow a woman to get raped is because she's filled with so much pride."

"Yeah, that's His way of humbling them."

She ignored them and went into the living room, closed the door and cried. She actually thought within herself that God had brought her to Baltimore to die, but then she thought that if He really wanted to kill her, He didn't have to bring her all the way to Maryland to do it. He could have killed her in Mississippi where she was.

Half an hour later, she went upstairs to the bathroom. Flashes of her life began to go through her mind. She remembered being molested for years by her older cousins. She remembered her mother burning her inner thighs with cigarettes and saying it was her fault for being clumsy. She remembered being raped and she remembered the abuse she suffered at the hands of men who claimed they loved her. She remembered being told throughout her life that she was nothing and would never amount to anything. She heard her mother's voice say that it was a waste for her to go to college and become educated because she wasn't going to amount to anything. She remembered her husband's brother trying to rape her and she thought about the stranger who attacked her the day before and made her lose her babies. She heard all of their voices ringing in her mind and she snapped.

"Shut up! Just shut up!" She said as she placed her hands over her ears. "Just leave me alone! I said shut up!"

Alexander and his mother came running up the stairs. They banged on the door.

"Baby, are you alright? What's going on in there? Open the door!" Alexander yelled.

"Evette, open the door. What's wrong in there?" His mother said.

Alexander kicked the door in, grabbed her and held her in his arms. "It's going to be okay. Calm down. Everything is going to be alright."

"Make them shut up, Alexander. Please make them stop talking."

"There is no one in here but you, baby. No one is talking. It's okay."

"Don't you hear them? Why can't you hear them?"

His mom touched his shoulder. "I think you'd better take her home."

"Yes, I think you're right." They got up to leave. His mom whispered in his ear.

"Don't let her call anyone. We'll handle it. I'll make sure she gets the help that she needs. Just keep quiet and pray to God."

Alexander had to take a couple of days off from work to take care of his wife. As his mother had instructed him, he kept her from making any phone calls. He had thought about having her committed in Spring Grove Mental Institution in Catonsville, Maryland, but decided against it. The only thing that kept her from committing herself was the fact that she didn't know where the locations of any good mental institutions were.

That morning, Evette awakened to find herself wrapped in Alexander's arms. He'd held her all night. She nudged him.

"Alexander, wake up." She shook him a little. "Alexander, baby, please wake up. A.J. is crying."

"No he isn't. Go back to sleep."

"Yes, he is. I hear him. How can you lay here like this while your son is crying his eyes out?"

"If it will make you feel better, I'll go check. Okay?"

"Fine."

He got out of the bed and went into the area of the living room where A.J.'s crib was. Their son was soundly sleeping. He went back into the bedroom, climbed in bed, and held his wife.

"I told you, he's asleep."

She began to cry. "Alexander, what's happening to me? I know I heard him. I heard him just as plainly as I hear you right now."

He squeezed her in his arms. "Don't worry about it; everything is going to be alright." He began to pray for her and ask God to heal her mind.

As the months flew by, Evette became more and more withdrawn. One night, they were visiting New Shiloh Temple, in Randallstown, Maryland and when the altar call was made, Evette went up for prayer. She was never the type that allowed just anyone to pray for her. She had to respect you and she had to believe that you could get a prayer through. She went to the Pastor's wife, Evangelist Newton.

"What do you need from the Lord, child?"

"I need you to pray for me that God will free me from the spirits of fear and depression."

"Well, the Bible says in II Timothy 1:7 that God has not given us the spirit of fear but of power and love and of a sound mind. What are you afraid of?"

"They made me promise not to tell."

"They who?"

"My in-laws."

"Come with me." She led Evette into the Bishop's office. "I knew something was going on with you and that family. My husband and I got saved at St. Andrews and our children grew up with the Worthington children. We know that family all too well. I want you to know, first of all, that you can trust me. What ever you say to me is between you and me. The only way I'll mention it to someone else is if I know they can help you better than I can. Okay?"

"Yes, ma'am. Well, it all started…" She told her the whole story and left nothing out. She didn't try to make them look bad and she didn't try to make herself look good. She just told it like it was. Evangelist Newton wrapped her arms around her and began to cry.

"You poor, poor child." Then it dawned on her. "Oh, my God. I have to tell my husband."

"But you promised."

"I know, but you have to understand, Marvin comes here all the time and what if he should try to assault one of the sisters in our congregation? I know I have to protect your confidences, but I'm also obligated to do whatever I can to protect the members of this church as well. Do you understand?"

"Yes, ma'am. I do."

"Evette, have they tried to get you the help that you need?"

"No, ma'am. Evangelist Worthington said that she would take care of it and see to it that I got help, but she's done nothing thus far."

"And she's not going to do anything. That family has more secrets then the F.B.I. Don't worry about it. I'll help you. Do you know Michelle?"

"Your Minister of Music? Yes, ma'am, but not in a personal way."

"Well, by profession, she's a counselor. She specializes in women's issues. I'm going to talk to her and see if she can force you into her schedule. Don't worry about the money. She'll do anything for me."

Evette gave her a big hug, thanked her and left out of the office. Alexander's mom saw her coming out and knew that she'd just disclosed the events that had taken place. Evangelist Newton went straight to her husband, pulled him off to the side of the pulpit and told him what had happened to Evette. Next she went to Michelle and told her. Bishop Newton approached her and gave her a hug.

"My wife just informed me of what you've been through. We are very much aware of the type of family you married into and I want you to know that if you ever need someone to talk to, you can always come to me." He shook his head. "It would be to your advantage if you left that church. I'm not trying to tell you what to do, but we can help you over here."

Sister Michelle and the Bishop's wife walked up. Turning to them, Bishop continued.

"Evangelist Worthington, this is Sister Michelle Mason. You know her as our Minister of Music but she is also a professional counselor dealing specifically with women's issues." They shook hands.

"Praise the Lord, Evangelist Worthington. Evangelist Newton was just telling me a little bit about your issues. I must say that it is not uncommon that a lot of sexual misconducts occur within families. I'm sorry you've had to keep this locked in for so long, but the good thing is that you're getting the help you need now. Are Fridays at noon good for you?"

"I'm a house wife, so anytime that's good for you is good for me. I'm not going anywhere."

She gave Michelle her address and phone number, they exchanged embraces and left.

By now, she'd stopped praying, fasting and reading the Bible. She felt as though God had forgotten about her and she no longer trusted Him to protect her from her front door to the steps; ten feet. She stayed locked up in the apartment with A.J. She kept the windows down and the blinds closed. She wouldn't even take A.J. outside in the front yard to play. She was too afraid that God would allow something terrible to happen to them and she didn't want to risk it.

The buzzer went off. She ran fearfully over to the window to see who it was. Michelle saw her, smiled and waved. She buzzed her in.

"You have it very nice in here."

"Thank you. You can have a seat on the couch."

She sat down slowly as she looked around the apartment. "I can tell that you are a very intelligent person."

"How is that?"

"Because of the way you have your apartment decorated."

Evette frowned. "I don't get it. What does that have to do with anything?"

"May I look in your closet?"

"Sure." Evette began to wonder what sort of help Michelle would be able to provide.

"Just as I thought."

"Is something wrong, Sister Michelle?"

"All of your clothes are arranged in the closet facing the same direction and they are all hanging in a color coordinated pattern."

"And what does that say about me?"

"Also, your apartment is decorated in a way that one area automatically blends or leads into the next and everything is meticulous."

"I still don't get it?"

"It says that you are intelligent, organized, passionate, a thinker and a planner and that you take your time to do things right."

"All that in ten minutes. You're good."

"Now that we've broken the ice, shall we begin?"

She took the seat that Evette had instructed her to take on the couch and Evette sat across from her in the matching white, soft leather chair. She watched how Evette moved. She was like a stallion whose spirit and will had just been broken. When Evette sat down in the chair, she was slumped over and almost balled in a knot. Sort of like how an abused puppy curls into the corner of a room when it's afraid of being hurt again. Michelle took out a notepad and pencil to take notes.

"Evette, tell me, how did you and Minister Worthington meet?"

"We met during the National Convention." Her face lit up slightly and she cracked a faint smile. "One year later, we were engaged and one year after that we were married. The rest, as they say, is history."

"I remember your testimony about conceiving A.J. You must be pretty grateful."

A.J. was crawling around and trying to pull himself up on the entertainment center.

"I feel blessed." Evette stated.

"How are you feeling about God these days."

The small talk was over. Now they were getting to the issues as hand.

"I don't really feel anything about God these days." Evette replied.

"Oh, come on. Surely, you do. Aren't you upset with Him? Don't you feel that He's forgotten about you? What is going through your mind about Him?"

"Okay, honestly? I feel pissed off with Him. I trusted Him and He failed me. He let me down just like He's always done throughout my life." She began to cry and she dropped her head in shame for what she'd just blurted out.

"Evette, the only thing that is truly going to help you obtain victory over what has happened to you, is if you acknowledge how you feel about God first of all and then allow forgiveness to come forth. I know it's hard but because you said that God has always let you down, I want you to tell me all of the experiences you've had where you feel He disappointed you. Go back as far as you can remember."

"I don't think I can." Evette cried.

"I know it's painful to think about all of the mean and hurtful things that we've been through, but I've discovered that it does bring forth healing. You can begin whenever you like."

She took a deep breath and allowed her mind to go back in time. She shook her head. "I really can't do this."

"Yes, you can. You're a lot stronger than you think you are."

"No, I'm really not." Evette denied.

"Yes, you are. You had to be in order to have made it this far." Michelle encouraged.

After about five minutes of non-stop crying, Evette finally regained some semblance of composure and she began.

"As far back as I can remember is when I was five years old. My sister was four and my brother was three." She paused.

"Keep going."

"That's when my memory began of our older cousins molesting us." She paused again.

"It's really not uncommon for those who have been molested to marry into a family of molesters. Keep going."

"You see the thing about it is that it was our older female cousins that were molesting us. They did everything from fondling to performing and forcing us to perform oral sex. This went on for years. It didn't end until I was ten years old. That's when I found out that what they were doing to us was wrong. You see, my mom never allowed us to really associate with anyone outside of the family for fear that we'd be hurt. She didn't realize that it was the family that was hurting us." She continued.

"Before we found out it was wrong, we had grown accustomed to it and almost looked forward to it, the attention, the comfort of it all, especially me because I felt like my mother hated me."

Michelle asked, "Why would you think that your mother hated you?"

"Because I reminded her so much of my father. They'd gotten a divorce and he went off to start his own business but he never did anything for us. She took it out on me, because I reminded her of him. She always said I was just like my no good daddy. I still have the cigarette burns on the insides of my thighs from where she'd burn me and then say it was my fault for being so clumsy." You could feel the bitter resentment as it filled the air. "And it was God who let it all happen. If He wouldn't protect me as a child, why should He be any different towards me now that I'm an adult?"

"Why do you blame God for what happened?"

"Even though we weren't raised in church, my mother always told us that the Devil was bad and that God was good and nothing can happen to you except God allows it. He allowed it, so it's His fault."

"What happened during your life when you were between twelve and fifteen?" She kept writing.

"By the time I turned twelve, I'd already been the victim of an attempted rape. Two boys in my class tried to rape me after school. The only thing that stopped them was when this other little boy who had a crush on me jumped in to save me. While they were beating him up, I had the chance to get away."

"You don't think it was God who allowed that little boy to put himself on the line to save you from being gang raped?"

"No. It was God who allowed them to try to rape me in the first place. Anyway, by the time I turned twelve we moved back to Mississippi. A month after my fifteenth birthday, my mom told my sister and me that we only needed men for sex and we didn't even have to have that. She taught us to be independent. She told my brother the same thing about women. Shortly after that, I decided that if that was all men were good for, then why should I wait until marriage. That was undoubtedly the worst decision I've ever made in my life."

"What about between the ages of seventeen and twenty one?"

"When I was seventeen, one of the most horrid experiences that I had was when my mother found one of my lovers in my closet. She almost stabbed him with an ice pick and would have if he wasn't the best runner we had on our track team. After he ran out of the house, she beat me. That wasn't even the worst thing about it. It was what she said to me that left me feeling broken. She grabbed me by my hair and dragged me down the hall to her bathroom and made me look at myself in the mirror. She asked me what I saw and then told me I saw nothing. She said that I was nothing and that I was never going to be anything. Then she ripped up my ACT papers and said that it was a waste for me to be educated because I wasn't going to be anything anyway."

She continued. "By the time I turned eighteen, I'd already been stalked by an ex-lover for two years, not the one who was in the closet. This guy would beat me and force me to have sex with him. By the time I turned twenty, I'd already experienced two more abusive relationships and at 20 ½ years old, I got saved. Six months later, I was raped, his words, by my first boyfriend in church. When we went to confession, he made it seem as though I had seduced him and thus it was my fault. The pastor believed him and said that because of his honesty, he was not going to disfellowship us. Can you believe it? He throws me on the bed, I'm crying and begging him to stop, but yet he says I seduced him!"

By the time she got the last statement out, she felt as if she'd just finished fighting and was drained of all strength. However, to her surprise, in spite of the pain, talking about it did seem to give her a sense of relief.

"Our time is up and I think this is a great place to close until next week. I have an assignment for you this week."

Assignment? I didn't think I'd have to do assignments. "What is it?"

"I want you to take this." She handed her a composition book. "This week, I want you to write down every positive thing that has ever happened to you in your life. Like today, I want you to go as far back as you can remember. Okay?"

"Okay."

"Now, I want you to dismiss us with prayer."

"I can't. I can't talk to Him right now."

"Yes you can and you will because in the end, God is the only one that has the power to heal you."

She dropped her head and began. "Father, in the name of Jesus, thank you for the opportunity to heal. Thank you for Michelle and the gift that she is to the body of Christ.

Thank you for our time together and hopefully some good will come out it. In Jesus' name, amen."

Michelle gave her a hug. "Now, that wasn't so bad and I think you did quite well to say it's been a long time. Don't forget your assignment and one more thing; make love to your husband tonight. It's as much for you as it is for him. The last thing you want is for the two of you to be driven further and further apart. It's time to start mending."

Evette closed the door behind her. She looked at the composition book, picked up a pen and began to write every good thing she could think of. She remembered going to the studios in Chicago and taking family portraits. She was such a beautiful child despite the fact that she was dreadfully thin. She thought of her sister, Tajuan and her brother Eugene and how cute they were that day, too.

Next, she wrote of when her mother threw her a party for her sixth birthday. For the first time, she let them invite the other children from the neighborhood. She remembered having so much fun eating, laughing, and jumping double-Dutch. She began to smile at the thought of it.

Then she remembered her first crush. His name was Robert and he was in her cousin Kayla's class. She'd assisted her cousin in writing a skit for her eighth grade graduation and he sung during the intermission. The song he chose was called *Always and Forever*. Evette sat amazed.

She felt as if they were the only ones in the room and he was singing to no one but her. They never even spoke to each other but she felt as if he belonged to her for the months that followed. *I wonder where he is now?* She wondered.

She thought of the time she won first place in her school's speech contest and went on to compete in the nationals. She was given James Weldon Johnson's version of *The Creation* to learn. She saw herself pacing her back yard in Chicago with the paper in her hands learning it line by line. She was only eight years old, but when the time arrived, out of thousands, she came in second place. First place went to a young boy who did excerpts from Martin Luther King, Jr.'s speech *I Have a Dream*. As good as she was, he was better, but she was just glad to have placed. The next year she won again at her school and went again to compete in the National. *There is no feeling like being awarded for a job well done.* She thought.

She recalled all of the Christmases she'd experienced while growing up. Every year, no matter how bad times were, they always got everything they wanted for Christmas. Her mom worked hard to see to it that they didn't feel the full effects of being poor. She remembered the year that her mom lied to them and she actually laughed out loud at the thought. It was during the time that President Carter was in office and the nation was dealing with a hostage situation that was causing him to lose his popularity. A new guy, a former Hollywood actor named Ronald Reagan had stepped on the scene and was giving Carter a run for his money. Times were getting hard and their mom thought she wasn't going to be able to get them anything for Christmas. There is no worse feeling than what you get when you see the look of utter disappointment in the eyes of your child. So, instead of telling them the truth, that she didn't have any money, she told them that Santa Claus was mugged on the L.

She always made them watch the news before they went to bed and that night, sure enough, there was a segment that talked about Santa Claus being mugged on the

L. Of course, it was one of those people who represent the Salvation Army, but they were too young to know that. However, when Christmas came, through the miracle of borrowing money from a friend, they had everything they'd asked for.

She smiled as she thought of how her mother always found a way to make things all right. She never compromised her integrity. She never lowered her standards. She was a woman of great principle.

That's enough for now. I need to get dinner started. She went into the kitchen and began preparing her husband's favorite meal. *This should be a pleasant surprise for him.* She cooked spinach, baked macaroni and cheese, homemade candied yams, and fried chicken. She also made lemonade. She thought of how Alexander had a serious sweet tooth. *Lord, you know I don't know how to bake. You know everything about everything including how to bake. Help me to surprise my husband with some...* She looked around the kitchen to see what she had. *Some homemade oatmeal cookies.*

By the time Alexander arrived home from work, the table was spread and Evette had baked four-dozen cookies. She greeted him at the door with a big hug and kiss.

"Where is all of this coming from?" He asked.

"Don't worry about it. Just be glad that it finally arrived."

His bath water was awaiting him. She undressed him, he climbed in the tub and she washed his back. As was her routine, when he was ready to eat, she served him. When she finished cleaning the kitchen, she made love to him. Flashes of her assaults ran through her mind, but she managed to push them all aside.

They had a wonderful evening together. The next day, Evette continued writing in the composition book. She remembered her days of being in the coronation balls, being an original member of a start-up singing group they called *Angel's Touch* in the 8th grade and how the group dominated the talent shows until she and the last three members graduated. She thought of when she was the first Miss French in her school in over twenty years and she was Miss Cheerleader.

It was then that she realized that even though the bad times were bad, the good times were better and more than she had remembered. She began to see things differently, not necessarily better, just differently.

The phone rang. "Hello." She answered. It was Sister Denise Axel.

"Praise the Lord, Sister Axel." Evette continued. "I'm not catching you at a bad time, am I?"

"Oh, no. Your timing is fine. What can I do for you?" Evette could tell that she was crying.

"You just came across my mind and I decided to call. Are you all right?"

"Actually, no I'm not." Sister Axel broke down.

"Is there anything I can do for you?" Evette asked.

"No. I can't really talk right now. I'm on my way out the door."

"Where are you going?" Evette asked.

"Over to my girlfriend's house."

"Is she one of the sisters in another church?"

"Actually, she's not saved."

"Why are you going over there then?"

"Because I need to get away."

"Look, you can come over here. With whatever is going on with you right now, I don't think being around an unsaved person is the best thing for you."

"I don't wanna inconvenience you or Minister Worthington."

"Really, it's fine. If folks in the church can't be there for one another who else will? I know how far you live from me, so I'll be expecting to see you within the next fifteen minutes. If you hurry, you can catch the next bus."

"I'm on my way."

Fifteen minutes later, Denise arrived and with her was their youngest son Jamal. He was about three weeks younger than A.J. The year they were born, every sister in the church who could get pregnant had gotten pregnant and they were all just a few weeks apart. She came in with a diaper bag full of clothes, diapers and bottles filled of milk.

"My, my, my." Evette said. "Looks like someone is trying to run away." And she gave her a big hug. Denise fell to the floor crying like a baby.

"I can't take it anymore. I know I'm not the best person in the world and I've done my share of wrong, but I deserve better than this."

Evette held her in her arms and rocked her back and forth as they sat on the floor together. "Hush now. Calm down. It's going to be all right. Calm down. You don't want to upset the baby."

It was almost half an hour before Denise was able to calm down.

"Would you like to talk about it?" Evette asked.

"Not right now."

"Okay. We can watch some videos and when you're ready to talk, we can."

She put in tapes of her favorite sermons. First there was Evangelist Jackie McCullogh's *The Ability to Recognize Jesus* and then she put in *God Will Get You There* and finally they watched the last concert she'd ministered in with her choir in Mississippi before she married Alexander. After all of that preaching and singing, Denise was ready to talk.

"Evangelist Worthington…"

She interrupted. "No. Please call me Evette."

"Evette, I just don't understand. I try to be a good mother and a good wife, but how can I get my husband to appreciate me and take care of the children? If he wasn't ready to be a husband and a father, he should never have asked me to marry him. Our house is falling apart, we don't have any food, our children need clothes and shoes and he's content just going to church and praising God as if something is going to fall from the sky and make everything all right. I'm tired of this. I've been going through this for six years now and I'm sick of it. I deserve better than this.

My children deserve better than this." She began to hyperventilate and Evette ran and got a small, brown paper bag out of the kitchen, and ran over to her.

"Calm down. Breathe into this. Calm down Denise. I know you're fed up mentally and emotionally, but getting sick physically is not going to help your situation. Now, you've got to calm yourself down. Have you spoken with the Pastor?"

"Yes, but it hasn't done any good."

As much as she didn't want to ask it, she did. "Have you spoken with the Lord?"

"No."

"Well, let's do that much at least."

They began to pray and cry out to God. Evette heard some of what she was saying.

"God, just kill me. I can't live like this. If you're not going to help me than I might as well be dead."

Evette wrapped her arms around her. "Oh, God, no! She can't die right now. She has five children to raise and she has her own destiny to fulfill. Please forgive her emotionalism of the moment and bless her." They both cried. Evette thought to herself *here I am interceding for someone else and I need help myself. God, why is it that you seem to have those who need help, helping others?*

By the time they finished, Denise felt a lot better. Then the phone rang. Evette answered it. It was Denise's husband Lance. He said that God told him that Denise was there. "Man, please. God didn't tell you anything. It was a matter of deductive reasoning. There are only three people in the church that your wife associates with - Sister Bogess and her cousin, Sister Brandy, and me. Her cousin isn't home and Sister Bogess lives to far away. It just made sense that she would be with me since I'm only a fifteen minute bus ride up the street."

"May I speak to my wife, please?" He said sternly.

"Hold on." She walked over and handed her the phone. "It's Lance. He wants to speak to you."

By this time, she had some strength and when she hung up, she was ready to go home. Evette gave her $50 for some food and she gave Evette a big hug.

"Thanks for praying with me. I think I'll be all right now. Even if the situation doesn't change right away at least now I have some grace to hang in there until it does."

"You're welcome. Just know that if you ever need me, I'm here."

They gave one another a final hug and Evette closed the door behind her. *I guess needing help is no reason for not giving help*, she thought.

When Alexander arrived home, dinner was ready and the table was set. His clothes were ironed and had been laid across the bed. It was a church night. Evette and A.J. were already dressed and ready to head out the door. He rushed through dinner, took a quick shower, got dressed and they headed out to pick up the saints for church.

Evette hated picking up the people for church. They were never ready when the van arrived and seldom did anyone give anything towards gas. They had drained their savings account from picking up people for church. To make matters worse, when services were over, the people never went directly to the van so that Alexander could take them home. The result was that they never got home before midnight and Alexander would end up getting no more than three and half hours of sleep because he had to get up for work at 4a.m. *People can be so inconsiderate.*

By the time they arrived at church, service was already under way. Evette headed straight for the back and sat down with A.J. Service was typical and when it was over, the same people who always came to the altar for prayer were the same ones that came that night.

"Alexander." His mother called.

"Yes, mom."

"How has Evette been doing lately?"

"She's fine. She started her counseling sessions with Sister Michelle the other day and.."

She cut him off. "She started what?"

"She started her counseling sessions."

"That's what I thought you said. Well, you have a good night."

"Good night to you to, mom."

She watched him as he headed out toward the van and thought *I'm going to have to put a stop to that.*

Unknown to either of them, this was to be their final session. No one knows how Alexander's mom put a stop to it, but she did.

"Hi Evette." Michelle said as she entered the apartment.

"Hi. Come on in and have a seat."

"This is going to be our last session."

Totally shocked, she asked, "Why?"

"I don't really know. I was just told that this would be our last time meeting. I want you to know that I feel you have made a lot of progress and I think that from here on out, you're going to be just fine."

"If you say so."

That afternoon was filled with talk of mending the relationship between her and her husband. When Michelle left, she handed Evette a series of tapes by Bishop T.D. Jakes entitled *Woman Thou Art Loosed.* This time, Michelle said the final prayer. It would be years before Evette would see Michelle again because shortly after their last counseling session, she and her husband left their church and started a ministry of their own. All of this happened after God delivered Michelle from her own demons. *Man, I would never have guessed that she was struggling with an issue like that.* Evette thought. Elder Bogess made it a point of letting Evette know Michelle's business. After all, the best way to keep someone Isolated is to destroy their trust in everyone around them.

Three weeks later, around 6p.m., the doorbell rang. It was Alexander's mother. They were both home. One of his younger brothers and his girlfriend was there also. Donald and Linda knew from the very beginning what Alexander and Evette had been going through as far as the spirit of infidelity.

Linda, who was a virgin and had been saved since early childhood, made it a point of verbalizing her utter disgust in Evette. Yet, she also continued to speak to who God had called and anointed Evette to be. She would often say, "Yes, you're a mess right now, but you're still God's anointed and you're going to be all right. One day, you are going to look back on this and use it to help others." Every time she would speak to Evette she would speak to who she was in God, not by what she was manifesting. "Praise the Lord, holy woman of God. How is the Evangelist doing today?" And Evette's soul would ache, because who she was to become was not who she was at that time.

Evette opened the door. Evangelist Worthington looked at her, burst into tears and then they all began to weep. She looked around the room and asked, "Donald, did you know?" He nodded his head. She looked across the room. "Linda, you knew, too?"

Linda nodded her head and said, "Yes, ma'am. I knew from the very beginning, in January."

"Alexander, you too?"

"Yes, ma'am." He answered.

Evette tried to reach her hand out to her mother-n-law and she hardened. If the shoe were on the other foot, Evette would have slapped herself. She raised her hand up to Evette and shook her head. "I'm tired of crying today. My heart can't take it anymore." And she left, wailing and calling on the name of Jesus. Evette closed the door and they all began to wail and cry and pray. To make matters even more challenging, Alexander had been invited to preach at a church that same night.

He talked about sin and its repercussions. By the time he sat down, everyone was on their feet praising God. Evette sat there crying. She was proud of him for having been strong enough to push past the issues at hand and deliver the word of God as if nothing was going on. When they returned home, he asked her to make love to him and she did.

The months that followed were virtually unbearable. Evette wouldn't have wished them on her worst enemy. The pastor and his wife began to make phone calls telling everyone what Evette had done. Before she knew it, the entire organization, seemingly, knew what had happened.

When she asked him about it, he said he had the right to *warn* the congregation. Yet, at the same time there was another situation of equal measure that the family was keeping silent and just as Evette had predicted, he told everyone that she had seduced him and he was a victim. Everyone that had any sense knew better, but Evette was the newcomer. She was older. She was married and somehow the latter fact meant that Evette was not supposed to have any problems. She was supposed to be above temptation. She was supposed to be beyond human, but marriage is not a cure-all for deep seeded emotional and psychological needs.

A pastor that was familiar with the family suggested that Evette go to her mother-in-law and personally apologize to her. At first, she didn't want to open her bedroom door but reluctantly, she came out. She, Alexander and Evette went into the living room to talk.

"I know I don't have any right to ask you this, but I wanted to say that I'm sorry and ask you to forgive me." Evette said.

She sat sternly. Her eyes seem to pierce right through Evette, but there was nothing to see. "What happened? I want to know everything." Evette told her everything exactly the way it happened. She didn't try to make anyone look bad and she didn't try to make herself look good. She just told it like it happened. She looked at Alexander, "So, what do you think about what your wife has done?"

"What my wife has done?" He said. "What about what my brother has done. He was my brother long before she became my wife."

She turned back toward Evette. "Evette, how could you allow a whorish spirit to come upon you like this? This, this spirit of Jezebel! I don't know if you will ever be able to be saved. I don't know if God will ever forgive you for what you've done. Alexander," she said as she looked at him, "you know you can get a divorce, right?"

Before she went any further, Evette said, "I know what happened with Raymond and Denise." Her countenance immediately changed.

"Well, God is a forgiving God." She changed up really quickly.

"Oh," Evette said, "So, now that I've made you aware that I know what else is going on in the family, now you say that 'God is a forgiving God.'"

"Well," she shook her head and looked at Alexander, "can you forgive your wife for this?"

"I already have, mom."

"Lord, have mercy." She let out a sigh. "I guess if you two can make it through this, you can make it through anything."

They left.

They thought that it would end right there, but it didn't. They wanted to have a meeting at the church with all parties involved. This they did with Evette only, not with the other members of the family who had committed the same sin. The meeting was to be held at the church and Evette felt as if she was going before the judgment seat of Christ. She already knew that she was the villain. She already knew what everyone thought. They just wanted to satisfy a sick tradition that had been taking place in some churches for years. They wanted details. Only God knew why.

Evette had asked a Bishop from another organization that she trusted to be present because she wanted an unbiased opinion at her 'trial.' Also, Bishop Langley, because he had a revival to preach and couldn't be there, had asked a wife of one of the Elders to be present on his behalf. The two of them along with Alexander's brother sat on the left side of the church near the doors. Elder Bogess stood in front of them while his wife sat in the back. Alexander's mother and father sat together near the center of the church and Alexander and Evette sat beside each other toward the front.

So, there they were and with the judge, jury, perpetrators and character witnesses all present and accounted for, and thus Evette's 'trial' began. She felt like the woman who was caught in the act of adultery whom the Pharisees brought before Jesus so he could sanction them stoning her to death. In that story, the religious leaders took the woman so she could be put to death, but they left the man in the bed. For whatever reason, they chose to leave the man alone and only kill the woman.

Elder Bogess began his opening statements. "First of all, I want to know why you are here." He demanded of the sister. Earlier, Alexander and Evette had told them that Bishop Vance would be coming. That made them all very upset, but they told them they wanted an unbiased person in the room.

"I'm here because Bishop Langley asked me to be here in his stead." She answered.

"Oh, my God, Bishop Langley knows." It was Alexander's mother. She looked at Evette. "Who else have you told?"

"I don't know how he found out. He called me last week, told me that he was made aware of the situation and asked me to tell him what happened and, unlike you all, he believed me. I didn't know he had planned on coming and I didn't know that he would send someone in his stead." Evette stated.

"Well, she's here now so let's move on." Elder Bogess interrupted. He looked at Evette and said, "Sister Evette, do you have anything to say for yourself?"

"No, sir. I don't think it would make any difference." She answered with her head hung. She felt as if her chin and her chest had become one.

"What about you?" He asked as he looked at Alexander's brother.

Bishop Vance interrupted. "If I may step in for just a moment." Elder Bogess nodded his approval. "Before this goes any further, has anyone, other than Alexander's wife, apologized to him? I just wanted to know, because if you haven't, then *that* is where you should begin." Apologies were made.

His brother was asked to give his version of what occurred. Evette only spoke up when he said something that wasn't accurate, which was most of the time.

"That nasty demon should be at the altar right now, begging God for forgiveness." Elder Bogess' wife shouted out.

"Well, if she's a nasty demon, what is he?" Bishop Vance interjected as he pointed across the room. "If she should be at the altar repenting, he should be right beside her. After all, she didn't do it alone. If one should repent, all should repent."

The pastor's wife continued. "Alexander, you never should have married that girl. She's brought shame and disgrace upon the whole family. You need to divorce her!"

Bishop Vance, "It appears to me that this family has had issues long before these two ever met, let alone got married. And we need to be careful how we tread on God's territory. If Minister Alexander wants to keep his marriage in tact, than anyone who tries to come between that will have to answer to God, because the Bible says that those whom God has joined together, let NO man put asunder. I have to admit, he's a better man than I am and probably the most saved person in this room right now."

Elder Bogess, "Alexander, do you have anything to say about this situation?"

He cleared his throat and proceeded to turn his back toward Evette as he faced his family. "Yes, I do. First of all, I want to say that I forgive all of you. Secondly, I believe that this is just a trick of the devil to bring division into the family, but we can't let him win. I think we all need to move forward and try to heal from this."

They all sat there crying and by the time the meeting ended, everyone was hugging and embracing each other as Evette sat on the side watching. They had come to the conclusion that the Devil was trying to destroy the family. Evette guessed that meant she was the tool being used.

She resented the fact that she had been blamed as the cause of the family's issues and yet, at the same time, she felt that she was getting the treatment that she deserved. She felt that this was God's way of punishing her for her sins. Surely nothing could have been worse, other than death itself. There is nothing like being left at the hands of church folk who want to see you die. They just didn't know, at that time, no one wanted death more than Evette did.

She was floored by what her husband had said. In her eyes, he had sided with his family. Did she expect him to side with her? No, of course not, but she didn't expect him to side with them either. To her, there were no sides to take because they were all wrong.

As the weeks passed, she sank deeper into depression. She didn't want to eat and she only cooked because Alexander and A.J. needed to eat. She didn't want to answer the phone and she certainly didn't want to leave the apartment. However, when Sunday would come, she would still go to church. It was more out of habit than devotion. She sat in the back of the church, there but not there. Evette felt as if her soul had left her and all that remained was indescribable pain and emptiness. She felt, more than ever, isolated and lonely and she began to wish she'd never gotten saved.

One day, while lying in the bed contemplating suicide, she heard this distant voice say, "Evette, talk to me."

Aloud, she replied, "But I don't know what to say."

Again the voice said, "Talk to me."

She shook her head and cried. "I can't. You won't hear me if I did and I don't know what to say."

"Just say, 'Lord, help me.'"

She slowly drug her naked body out of bed and onto the floor. She laid there, face down and whispered her silent scream for help. The more she said 'Lord, help me' the more she felt the burden lift. The more the burden lifted, the more she cried out to Him. Finally, she mustered up the courage to do the one thing that she had stopped doing. She talked to God.

"Lord, God. I come before you now the same way that I came into this world, naked and alone. You made me and you know me. Before you laid the foundations of the Earth, you knew that I would arrive at this point in my life. So, here I am, God, and I can do nothing but what I did when I first came to you and that is to ask you to save me. Save me from myself. Save me from the ghosts of my past. Save me from the darkness that dwells within my soul. Wash me again, God, and make me whole. You never have to use me again. I never have to preach or teach or do anything for you again. I just want to be able to feel your presence. I

just want to be free to praise you. In Jesus' name, amen."
And she lay in that position for hours crying.

The next year became torturous at best. The mere
thought of going to church caused all joy to disappear.
Evette was told that she had to 'prove to the saints that she
had repented and changed.' This seemed beyond reasoning
since no one has a Heaven or a Hell to put anyone in. She
felt that if she and Alexander were trying to get through it
who were they to feel that she owed them anything? But in
a sense she did. She had brought a reproach upon God,
herself, her husband and the local assembly and even
though the other party didn't want to own up to his part in
it, she knew she had to. Not for them, but she had to go
through it for herself. She knew that if she could survive
the 'saints' she could survive anything.

Gradually, she began to regain some of the ground
that she had given away. Mentally, though, she was the
same. Evette did learn one very important lesson during
that period of her life, sometimes people just don't want to
see you get up and move on. The best thing about it is that
it's during those times that you find out what you are all
about. You strip away all of the hypocrisies, take off and
throw away all of the masks, and search for the 'you' that
got lost during your indoctrination process. In short, you
find out who God and you really are and, in time, you learn
to love Him, yourself, and others. You realize that God is
divine and you are human, full of faults and frailties and
subject to failure. You learn that any good thing that comes
out of you is not because of your great holiness or the
'works' that you are doing, but because of God's greatness
and the purpose that He has designed for your life as you
submit to HIS leading.

She was learning all of these things, while at the same
time labeling herself 'the sacrificial soul.' She felt as if her
soul had no value in the place she was at. She felt that she
was the decoy; the one that all attention was diverted to so
that no one could see what else was going on with the
Worthington family. But she always believed that some

things have a way of letting themselves out of the closet. The more the Worthington's tried to smear her, the more the rest of the family's business began to be revealed.

One day, one of the sisters from the church that Evette had encouraged for years, called her. She told Evette that she was praying for her and then she told her how that the pastor's wife had called her and told her to disassociate herself from Evette because she, as Sister Bogess said, might try to sleep with her husband. Evette called her a liar and told her she was just trying to dig for more dirt. The sister then proceeded to call the pastor's wife and told Evette to 'just sit and listen and don't say a word or I'll never talk to you again.'

Evette sat there, in silence, listening to the pastor's wife call her every name in the book. She made all sorts of accusations until finally; the sister said she had to go. "Stay away from that girl. I'm warning you." She continued.

"But Sister Bogess, what about what happened with Denise?" She asked.

"Bye, child." Sister Bogess hung up the phone without answering.

"See, I told you she was going around telling everybody your business and talking about you like a dog." She said.

Evette didn't know if saying 'thank you' was the proper thing to say at the time, but she did anyway. Later, she found out that the pastor was going around to the saints and telling them not to pray for her. He was telling them that they should not ask God to have mercy on her. One brother told her what his response was. "Now Elder Bogess, I think you're out of order. You can't go around telling folks not to pray for somebody. Isn't that what we're supposed to do when a brother or sister falls in sin? Besides, I know of people in this church who have done the same thing or similar and you didn't treat them nearly as bad as your treating her. Why is that?"

One-by-one, young couples began to leave the church. Evette was told that she was to blame, but she knew better.

Who could trust a leader who publicizes your confessions? Who could trust a leader, who, when you sin, not only tells everyone your business but also tells them not to even pray for you? She sat in silence and watched as the whole thing played out. She felt as if she had disconnected herself from herself and this was actually someone else's story she was seeing from a distance. But it was real and it was her.

Denise sank into a state of depression as well because by now, her sins had been publicized. No one knew how it got out, but Evette found out during a conversation with Linda, who by now had stopped seeing Donald. She didn't want to marry into a family with such deep-seeded issues and who could blame her?

One of Alexander's sisters, Denise, as it turned out, had had an affair with their sister Tanya's husband, Isaac during the time that Alexander and Evette were homeless. Evette would always see Isaac and Denise talking, but she thought nothing of it. Well, one time she did sense something, but she quickly dismissed it. This was two years before her incident occurred. The family was devastated, but they kept it quiet. After all, she was a Worthington and Evette wasn't. She was family and Evette was just an in-law.

When it all boiled down to it, after everything came out, the family told everyone that she was raped. In Evette's situation, she was the villain. In Denise's situation, Isaac was the villain. Thus, the family seemed to hold only in-laws responsible when something went wrong. Nothing was ever their fault and when it unmistakably was, it was downplayed as not being 'as bad as' what someone else had done.

Tanya couldn't handle the shame and embarrassment so she took their daughter and fled the state of Maryland. She also had her own inner demons to fight. Once, she had told Evette that there were years of her childhood that were gone from her memory. No matter how hard she tried, she couldn't, or wouldn't, get herself to recall any of those years. Evette was no psychologist, but she did know that sometimes when very traumatic experiences occur in our lives, our brains have a tendency of shutting down and not allowing us to recall it until we reach a point where we are ready to deal with it. Whatever she experienced that was so bad that her brain literally had to shut down as a mechanism of defense and preservation, Evette prayed that when it was revealed, she would be able to handle it.

For months, Isaac still lived in the house alone with Denise. She was in love with him and from all aspects of it he was in love with her, too. But how do you explain to someone that you're in love with your sister's husband? It sounds morbid, but incest is not as uncommon in the United States as some would like to think it is. As with the Worthington family, it is a silent secret that many families share. Sometimes things just have a snowball effect because while all of this was going on, Alexander was going through his own process. He had been molested as a child by one of his mother's brothers. He died a month before Alexander and Evette got married.

At the same time, a prominent Bishop in their organization was stripped of his Bishopric and disfellowshipped. He had been having an affair with the secretary of his church for years. She finally grew tired of it, and at the national convention, she came before the Board of Bishops and confessed every single gory detail of their relationship. She told that they'd had sex in the church office and the things he'd asked her to do just for him to get hard enough to penetrate her. When that came out, it rocked not only the churches that he presided over on the East Coast, but the entire organization. Know one knew the Bible like this man did, and yet it was the Bible that he used to get this woman to have an affair with him. He had used scripture references of concubines to do it. He convinced her that it was biblically okay for him to have her and be married to someone else at the same time.

He became the standard as far as referencing sin. "Well, you messed up, but at least you didn't mess up as bad as Bishop Johnson."

Lord, If You Don't Do It…..

During the process of time and a series of other events,
Alexander and Evette left the church. They felt as if they
were fleeing for their spiritual lives. Evette had asked
Alexander for a divorce because she was tired of fighting.
She was tired of being told that she wasn't good enough,
holy enough, gifted enough. She grew weary of mentally
fighting to stay afloat in church and she was ready to leave.
She was ready to leave God, the church, her husband and
even her son. Since she was unredeemable, so they taught,
she felt it was useless to continue trying.

God had dealt with Alexander about leaving in 1995,
but they were talked out of it. He spoke again in 1997, and
that time, they obeyed. The senior Pastors were Dr. Ronald
Davis and his wife Elder Angela Davis. That morning,
before they headed out, Evette prayed and told God that
she needed deliverance and that if He didn't do it, it just
wouldn't be done.

Unlike the church they had left which consisted of at
least sixty people, Dominion appeared to have about four
hundred members. She felt that it would be easy to 'get
lost' in the crowd there. She could just hide herself, come
and go unnoticed and live out the rest of her life in the
shadows of the church. Or so she thought.

The service was like nothing she'd ever seen before.
Instead of Praise and Testimony Service, there was
Worship Service where the people worshipped God for at
least an hour. As the Praise Team sang, there were about
eight ladies who danced. Evette watched as they moved in
harmony and she could see the genuineness upon their
faces. They were dancing before the congregation, but
mentally they were in the presence of God. She stood there
in awe and began to cry. She wanted to feel God's presence
again. It's a terrible thing to be in a place where God is
manifesting Himself and everyone is partaking of it but you.
Now she understood why David asked God not to cast him
away from his presence. Now she understood why Jesus

cried out 'My God, my God why hast thou forsaken me?' while he hung on the cross. Being disconnected from the presence of God while in the presence of God is a terrible feeling!

The Bishop got up and began to read the word of God. Then he began to cry and say what God was telling him. "I hear the Lord say, there's one person in this room today. You spoke to God this morning and you told God that if He didn't do it, it just wouldn't be done. I want you to some down to this altar right now. Come on. Come on. It's okay. God said He heard your prayers and He's waiting to receive you. Come now."

The moment he spoke, Evette knew that she was that 'one person'. It had to be God speaking through this man. He said the exact same words that she'd spoken just that morning to God. She reluctantly and fearfully stood up and began to make that long stretch to the altar. She confessed to the Bishop that she was the one. He asked her what she wanted God to fix in her life and she gave him a brief description of the events that had taken place in her life. She told Bishop Davis that God didn't have to ever use her again. All she wanted was to be free to praise God. All she wanted was to be able to feel the presence of God again and to worship Him.

"God said that there are others in here today with similar issues to this sister. You think that you can find what you need in other things and in other people to fill voids in your life. The reason nothing has worked is because that 'void' is a place that God Himself places within the hearts of mankind. It can ONLY be filled by and with Him. It's the place that God has reserved in us for Himself and Himself alone. Sex, can't fill it. Marriage can't fill it. Drugs can't fill it. Church can't even fill it. God said that what He's about to do for this sister is so powerful until others will be set free because of the overflow that's going to come from her. If I were you, I'd rush to the altar right now and jump in the overflow of this deliverance."

He laid hands on Evette. As he began praying for her, she was slain in the Spirit and fell to her face speaking in tongues and worshiping God. The altar filled with people who'd been using outside vices to fill the emptiness in their lives. Bishop Davis didn't preach that day, because God showed up and showed off. The morning service was turned into a deliverance service and prayer was the order for the day.

Evette had been saved long enough to know that she was in for a spiritual battle and that it wasn't going to be easy. She knew that the biggest enemies she had to conquer were herself, her past experiences, her present situation and the future that she'd grown to dread. She knew that she would have to admit that she had sexual issues that existed from childhood and had influenced her behavior until that day. She had no idea of the events that lie ahead, but at least now she was praying again, she was talking to God again and most of all, she could feel His presence again. No matter how many times she fell from this point on, she knew that in the end, she would come out victorious.

Financially, things were getting really bad for them. Though they continued to give 10% of their gross income to the church, they never seemed to be able to truly break even. Some people have a problem with paying tithes and offerings, but they believed the Bible when it says in the book of Malachi that you'd "be cursed" by God if you didn't do it. As hard as times were, they didn't want to risk things being made worse by disobeying the Word of God.

One day, a sister from St. Andrews told Evette that they could probably apply for food stamps. She scheduled the appointment and went in to fill out the paper work. After they'd taken her picture, they told her to come back within two hours so they could process her paper work. She walked over to one of the saint's homes and fellowshipped with them for a while. When she returned to the Social Security Office, a man approached her who was passing out flyers.

"Excuse me, Miss." She paused. "Do you want to learn more about computers?"

"Actually, yes."

"Take this and call this number. The name of the school is *Progressive Career Institute.* Good luck to you."

"Thank you." She looked up at the doors to the building and walked away. *If I can get through this program, I won't need assistance from the Government. Besides, I never liked the thought of getting help from Social Services anyway. Jesus is my help.*

She caught the bus to Edith's house and sure enough Alexander and their son were there. She showed him the flyer.

"Baby, I think we should go. What do you think?" She asked.

"I think it's a great idea. You can go during the day and I can go when I get off work in the evenings."

"But who will keep A.J. while I go?"

Edith interrupted even though Evette asked the question; she directed her response to Alexander. "Your father can keep him. He's home every day now since he's retired and you can pay him $50 a week."

"Pay him to watch his own grandchild? I've never heard of such a thing." Evette stated.

"Well, you can't get something for nothing." Edith replied.

Looking at her husband, Evette said, "That's *your* family."

Alexander got up and dialed the number. He scheduled their appointment for the next evening. For once, it seemed that things were beginning to look up for them.

Going Back to Work

Evette began to think that if she were to start working it would take her mind off of a lot of things and she could go to classes with Alexander at night. Alexander's mom suggested she call a temporary staffing agency. She looked in *The Baltimore Sun* and found one called *TBD Temporary Staffing*. Other than fast food, most of her work experience had been secretarial so that's what she went in to apply for.

She went for her appointment and passed the test with ease. They wanted her to come dressed the way she would dress at the office. They were impressed with her neatness and cleanliness. Evette always could make an excellent first impression. They hired her and sent her to a company in the county area of Maryland that makes certain foods and artificial flavors. She was sent there to perform data entry.

It was a pretty frightening job because her desk was surrounded by explosive chemicals. *We actually eat this stuff* she thought as she watched the men carefully extract liquids that, if accidentally spilled, could burn through the bones in your body. To make matters worse, there were rumors of a lot of the men being addicted to cocaine and other substances. *God, I hope none of these crazy people get upset and decide to poison the population. It would be rather easy to do, too.*

The assignment was short lived because one of the men felt on her leg while she was bent over tying her steel-toed boots in the break room. She reported him to Human Resources. Later, she discovered that he was the number one suck-up of all the white men there and before they tried to discipline him, they let her go. She learned a valuable lesson; sexual harassment is only disciplined when it's someone that everyone is out to get, but when it's the office pet, you can hang it up. She thought, *Sometimes it's better to keep your mouth shut.*

Two years later, she'd given birth to another baby. A little girl, that she named Eunice. She looked like a combination of Evette and her sister Tajuan. She even had a deep dimple in her right cheek, just like Tajuan. After Eunice was born, Evette went from one assignment to the next with the temporary agency. There were two places that really wanted to hire her but she kept having problems with baby sitters. It's amazing how people just want to see you down and suffering all the time. *The Galley*, a mall on the Inner Harbor that was owned by the Redding Company, wanted to hire her and her starting salary would have been $35 thousand. As soon as the sister from her church, who was keeping the kids, found out, all of a sudden she couldn't keep them any more. Evette ended up missing the job because she couldn't find a replacement in time.

During the summer of 2000, she and Alexander worked with the United States Census Bureau as Crew Leaders. They both supervised almost 30 individuals each and were responsible for quality control, making sure that the enumerators were putting forth a genuine effort at getting the data from the community members and not falsifying documents. They also performed payroll functions. They made some pretty good money from it, but not enough to pull them out of the financial hole that they had fallen in.

They were numbered among a large portion of Marylanders who had become victims of what was labeled a 'flipping' scam. The house was so messed up, until every lawyer that they had spoken to advised them to let it go. It wasn't worth saving. The person who swindled them, a fellow Christian, bought the house for $10,000 and sold it to them for $90,000. The house had lead paint in it, which they assumed contributed to A.J.'s diagnoses of ADHD (Attention Deficit and Hyperactivity Disorder), the roof over the sun parlor blew off, BGE told them that the electrical wiring in the house was a mess and could literally catch on fire without warning, the furnace system was completely rusted out and had been tagged by the fire department, whenever it rained, the water would seep into the wall structure and cause further electrical problems. They were literally living in a death trap. To make matters worse, by the time mid-September rolled around, Evette discovered – when the mortgage company called – that Alexander hadn't been making the mortgage payments and the house was being foreclosed on.

She would later find out that Alexander had conceived two other children by two different women during the same time that A.J. was born. All three children were born only months apart. This was one of many secrets that the Worthington family wanted to keep. This was why he didn't make that big a fuss over her indiscretion. This is why the family focused more on her, not just to draw attention away from Denise, but also to keep everyone's eyes of Alexander.

There was one bright spot, however. Two weeks later, on September 29th, the temporary agency she was employed with, sent her to an assignment interview at The Governor's Crime Prevention Office.

She was excited and nervous at the same time. *A branch of the Governor's office! What in the world am I going to wear?* She pulled out the $100 pair of shoes she'd purchased when she had an interview at Johns Hopkins. Even though it was the best interview she'd ever had and the woman really liked her a lot, she didn't get the job. It required her to travel between Maryland, DC and Virginia. They only had one car and Alexander used it to drive to his job at Fort Meade. *Okay. What can I wear with those shoes?* She really didn't have much of a choice since most of her things needed to be dry-cleaned. So she grabbed old faithful - a blue, two-piece skirt suit and a white silk blouse. *It doesn't make a 'power' statement, but it will have to do.*

Her interview was scheduled for 10a.m. Friday. She arrived around 9:30a.m. *It's better to be early than late,* she thought. The office was located just outside of Baltimore

City. The building was surrounded by a senior citizen complex. *Unless you knew this office was here, you'd never know this office was here.* She thought.

As she stepped off the elevator, she tried to make sure she didn't look desperate. *People don't hire folks who look desperate,* she told herself. She saw that the two doors were open. It was a quaint place. The receptionist, a while girl who looked all of twenty- one, sat at the desk. She had no choice but to acknowledge Evette because she came in smiling with her hand extended.

"Good morning. I'm Evette Worthington. I have a 10a.m. interview with Tad Scolia."

She looked her up and down and then proceeded to buzz Mr. Scolia.

"Tad. Your 10a.m. is here at 9:30a.m." She glanced up at Evette who was smiling at her. *Yeah, I caught your little snide remark, but it doesn't matter. I'm not here for you.* "Ms. Worthington," she interrupted her thoughts, "You can have a seat. Mr. Scolia will be with you momentarily. He's still interviewing another *temp*."

"Thank you." She took a seat on one of the burgundy, soft leather chairs. What the lady didn't know is that Evette saw her temporary agency time sheet sitting on the corner of the desk. *Why is she trying to front like she's a permanent employee when she's just a temp trying to get a break like me and the other lady in there?* "So how long have you been with the agency?" Evette asked and cracked a faint smile as she saw the look that came across the young girl's face. *Yup, you've been busted!*

"Well, I've just moved here a few months ago from Upstate New York, so this is my first assignment."

'Upstate New York'. I guess she wants to make sure I know that she comes from a family with money or something. I'm not impressed. Evette picked up a brochure about the agency and began reading it. The good part about coming early is that most places like these have stuff lying around that tells you all about the company. If you don't own a computer and you get there early enough, you have a

chance to read some of their materials and seem as though you know a little something about them.

"Thank you for you time and interest. Have a good day."

She lifted her eyes from the brochure to see a man she assumed was Mr. Scolia. He shook hands with the lady he'd just finished interviewing and she left out looking rather unconfident. She was sad and slouchy looking. In short, she looked desperate for a job. He approached Evette with his hand extended so she stood up, smiled and shook with a firm grip. He smiled, impressed by her handshake.

"Ms. Worthington, I assume?"

"Yes, I'm Mrs. Worthington." She placed extra emphasis on the word 'Mrs.' because she believed that governmental offices always prefer to hire people who are married. It cuts down on a lot of interoffice affairs, so they think.

"Follow me into the Executive Director's office. He's out today. The conference room is being used for a meeting and that's why we're in here. Have a seat."

He pointed to the chair closest to the door. She sat on the edge of the seat. She didn't want to get too comfortable because sometimes when she got too comfortable she had a habit of slouching in her seat. Evette felt that sitting on the edge kept her alert and in good posture.

The interview lasted all of twenty minutes and by the time it was over, they were on a first name basis. They got up from the table, shook hands, smiled at each other and left the office.

"Thank you for your time and interest." He said

He must have been rehearsing that all day, she thought. "You're welcome and thank you for *your* time and interest as well. I look forward to working with you, Tad."

She added a little shift in her hips as she exited the office. *Couldn't hurt*, she thought. She hoped she wasn't being too presumptuous by telling him that she was looking forward to working with him, but she felt she needed to speak a little faith concerning the situation. After all they had been through during the course of the past couple of years she needed to speak all the words of faith she could muster up.

Although things went well, she wasn't sure if she'd get the assignment or not. He'd made it a point of informing her that he still had a few more interviews left for the day. After she was out of the building, she headed to Burger King to get some lunch. She didn't eat breakfast that morning because she knew it would make her sluggish, so right about now she was famished. She ordered a cheeseburger BK Kids Meal and decided to eat in. Afterwards, she went down town to Charles Street to the Small Business Association building. She tried to study the different manuals that interested her, such as *How to Start Your Own Temporary Agency, How to Start Your Own Café, How to Become a Consultant and How to Write a Business Plan.* After several hours of reading, she decided she'd had enough and caught the bus home.

The voice mail light on the phone was flashing. After listening to the message two or three times, she finally let it all sink in. It was the temporary agency informing her that she had the position and would start on Monday morning, October 2nd at 8:30a.m. They asked that she call them when she got the message.

"Hello. Yes, this is Evette Worthington and I'm returning your call regarding the assignment with the Governor's Office."

"Oh, Yes, Evette. As I stated in the message, you'll start this Monday at 8:30a.m. Make sure you dress professionally since it is an Executive level position that is temp-to- hire. Have fun and don't forget to dress well." She hung up before Evette could go off on her. *Who does she think she is telling me something like that?*

When Monday arrived, she was there at 8a.m. She had to leave the house between 5:30 and 6a.m., take two buses and walk one block just to get there. She was wearing the $300 black and white, two-piece pants suit she'd purchased. She couldn't believe that it was a size 16/18. Even after dropping down from a size 22, she still felt as though she was caring another body around with her because when she and Alexander got married, she was a size 6/8. Evette was told that she was hired to support the Communications Team but they started her out on the phones. It was a twenty-line system and the white girl, Brenda, never gave her a chance to try using it, so Evette just watched and learned.

Brenda was blonde, not naturally though, was about five foot six, and was so thin, that you just wanted to treat her to an all-you-can-eat buffet or something. By the end of the week, she had made several 'race' and 'poverty' related comments, but it didn't matter because Evette was from the South, she could handle it. Once, when Evette was working in a nursing home for mental patients, a white lady spat in her face, cursed her out and called her all kinds of nigger this and nigger that's. Each time Evette wiped the spit from her face, the lady would spit again until finally, she saw that Evette was most certainly the stronger of the two of them and gave up. *Had that been about three years earlier, her racist tail would have been thrown out of the window,* Evette thought as she recalled the incident.

The following Monday, they hired a new receptionist. She and Evette hit it off immediately. Brenda had to teach her the phone system and just like she did Evette, she wouldn't let Leslie touch the phones. She had to watch. By then, Evette had been shown her cubicle on the other side of the hall and when the following Friday came, Brenda was informed that it was the last day for her assignment. They gave her no warning at all, but then to again, when you're a temp, they don't have to. At the end of the day, Brenda told Evette that she had a job lined up as a secretary for some legal firm. "Oh, yeah?" Evette asked. "Well, I hope things go well for you there." When they got off the elevator, Brenda reminded Evette that Wednesdays in Towson was Farmer's Market day and that she could pick up a lot of fresh fruits and vegetables for her family dirt cheap. "Thanks." Evette said. "I guess I'll see you around town."

Everyone was so nice and got along so well in the office, that Evette determined that this was where she wanted to be. People would stop by, lean over her partition and hold brief conversations with her and some even treated her to lunch a few times. One day, she was typing labels for some files and this guy named Baxter Jones approached her cubicle. Since he introduced himself as a future Senator, Evette introduced herself as a future multibillionaire. He smiled and told her that he liked the way she thought.

By the time she was entering her third week a lady named Anise approached her. She was African American, about five foot seven, of a chocolate complexion, dressed very well, but had a stank attitude.

"Are you the new temp?" She didn't ask, she demanded.

"Good morning." Evette pleasantly said as she extended her hand letting the lady know that manners do count to some people. Anise gave her a half-interested shake and asked again. "I said are you the new temp?"

"Well, yes I am and you are?" Evette asked.

"I'm Anise and I work with the Juvenile Accountability Grants. You will be working for me for three days and for the Communications Department for two.
The first thing I want you to do is this." She handed her some papers with names, phone numbers, and addresses on them. "These are the places that I need to go to for site visits. It's your job to set that up. I'll give you read and write access to my calendar today. Oh, by the way, what is your name?"

"My name is Evette and I thought I was brought in to work for Communications only."

"I'm sorry. You were misinformed. You'll be working for me for three days and working for Tad and Melissa for two. If they have a problem with that, tell them to come see me. Here you go." She said as she shoved the papers back in Evette's face and walked briskly away. *This chick has nerve and issues to match,* Evette thought.

"I see you've met Anise." An accented voice came from nowhere. She looked up and peeking over her cubicle was the young man who was seated in the area only twenty feet or so away from her. He was of a chocolate complexion and had to be all of five eleven. You could see his finely chiseled physique through his crisp white shirt. He extended his hand and they both exchanged firm grips. His smile was heart warming and his teeth were pearly white. You could tell that this was a brother that knew how to take care of himself.

"I'm sorry, because of your accent, I can't understand you."

"I said," He spoke slower, "I see you've met Anise. So what is your name?" He asked.

"*Mrs.* Worthington." She replied.

"Oh, you want to make sure I know up front that you are spoken for, huh? That's good. I like commitment in a woman." She wasn't sure how to respond to that last statement, so she didn't.

"And your name is?" She asked.

"Anthony. Anthony Shanung."

"So, what part of Africa are you from?"

"I'm from Nigeria."

"I'm of Ethiopian descent, myself." She informed him. "Well, Anthony, it was a pleasure meeting you."

"Trust me, the pleasure is all mine." He walked off and then suddenly returned. "Has anyone ever told you that you have the most exquisite eyes? They're quite captivating." And just as quickly as he came back, he left again, not giving her the slightest chance to dis him. Inside, though, she felt like jumping up and down. Someone had actually flirted with her as big and as out of shape as she was after giving birth to two babies and miscarrying five. A faint smile came from nowhere and found itself on her face. From that day forward, every time Anthony would see her, he'd warmly greet her with "Good morning or good afternoon Evette." Though his smile made her days, the attention was also a bit frightening.

"Evette, when you get a chance, can you come see me?" It was Melissa buzzing her on the intercom.

"Sure, I'll be right over." She responded.

Melissa was the part-time manager of the Communications Team. The Team consisted of two people: Melissa and Tad. She was about five foot five, white, with blonde hair. She was rather hyper too. Everything was urgent. Everything was an emergency, but she was kool and Evette liked her.

"Can you file some papers for me?"

"Sure thing." Evette responded.

"Wait a minute, before you do that, can we talk?"

"Okay." Evette took the burgundy leather seat by her desk and sat in it.

"Evette how old are you?"

"I'm thirty two."

"Tell me something about yourself."

Okay, she's interviewing me on the sly. "Well, I'm a graduate of Progressive Career Institute. I have six years of secretarial experience under my belt. I have good organizational skills, a typing speed of 65 words per minute, and a data entry speed of 13,000 keystrokes per hour or more, depending on how I'm feeling at the time. I have experience with Lotus 1, 2, 3, Lotus Notes, Excel, Word, Windows 95, 97 and 98. I have dicta phone experience…"

"Whoa, it looks like you have what I'm looking for. Why would you want to work here if at all?"

Evette cut straight to the chase because she was tired of playing games with people. "Because I need a job. I have two children and my husband's salary can't cut it alone."

Melissa was taken aback by her blatant honesty. "Well, I'll see what I can do. I am looking for someone permanent. I like you and I appreciate your honesty."

Evette stood up to leave. "Oh, Evette, one more thing. Are you a Christian?"

"No ma'am. I'm not a Christian, but I am a believer."

"Well, what's the difference?" Melissa asked.

"The word 'Christian' means to be Christ like. I'm not like Christ, Melissa. Sometimes I don't turn the other cheek. Sometimes I find it difficult to love my enemies or do good to those who despitefully use me. Sometimes I can hold a grudge and feel justified by doing it. So, I'm not like Christ. I'm a lot closer to it now than I was eleven and a half years ago, but I still have a long way to go."

"Hmm. I never thought of it that way before. Well, we'll have to talk later."

As the days went by, people came by her cubicle more and more, mostly to compliment her on a job well done. For some reason no one expected her to last as long as she did. Later, she discovered that Anise and Melissa had just gone through eight temps in a four-week period. Tad informed her that one chick only lasted half of the day. She said, around lunchtime, that she was going out to her car to get something and never came back.

"Girl, you must be some kind of special person or something." One lady said.

"Why is that?" Evette asked.

"Because you're working for the two worst people in the office to work for and you're still here. If you can work with Melissa and Anise, hell, you can work for any body."

After a while, the pressure began to take its toll on Evette. The foreclosure date was getting closer and they still hadn't found any place to move to. Evette knew that God always seemed to like doing things at the last minute so He could get the glory, but she was getting rather anxious. They had experienced being homeless before and she vowed that she would never go through that again. She knew that this time it would be worse. The first time, even though she was pregnant, it was just her and Alexander, this time it was them and two children. The thought of it caused her to run out of the office and go crying in the bathroom stalls.

"Are you all right in there? Is there anything I can do to assist you?" A voice came from another stall. It sounded familiar.

"No, I'm fine. I mean, I'll be fine." Then it dawned on her. *That's Marsha.* Marsha was one of the people who worked in the Programs Department and was known for throwing a mean party. She was Italian, about five foot nine, with long black hair and was well built despite the fact that she thought she was fat. *I hope she doesn't know that it's me in here. The last thing I need is for folks to start feeling sorry for me, or asking a bunch of questions.* However, it was too late. The office manager, had already seen her.

"Are you okay, Evette?" She asked. "I saw you run out the door and you looked like you were crying."

"I'm fine. Thanks for asking."

"I want you to know that I'm here if you ever need to talk. You *are* working for the two most difficult people in the office, you know."

"No, really. I'm kool." But she wasn't kool. Nothing was kool. She had been spending so much on gas, and daycare that she barely had money to dry clean her clothes, what few clothes she had. As the cold weather began to settle in, her wardrobe began to repeat itself. She found that she had to wear the same things two and sometimes three times a week. She would just mix them up. You know how it works. You wear the same pair of pants Monday and Wednesday but just change the color of the blouse you wear with it. Then you wear the same skirt on Tuesday and Thursday and change the color of your blouse with that. Friday was dress down day, so she wore casual pants and a T-shirt or a sweater. Of course, it wasn't too long before people began to notice that she was struggling.

"What are you doing for lunch today?" It was Anthony, peeping over her partition the way he usually does. *He probably noticed that all this week I've been eating bologna and crackers and drinking water for lunch.*

"Why? What's up?"

"Well, there is this nice oriental place at Towson Town Center and I was thinking that maybe I could treat you to lunch today. So, how about it?"

"Well, I don't know. I am married you know."

"So that means you can't eat? Come on, we'll have fun and it will definitely be a welcome change of scenery instead of you sitting here not ever getting up except to go to the rest room or get water."

"So you've been watching me, huh?"

"Well, I can't help it. You are within my eye's view and, besides, you have to pass by me every time you go to the sink. Remember?"

She smiled. "I really don't have any…"

He cut her off. "It's my treat. A real man never asks a woman to lunch or dinner and then makes her pay for her own food." *'A real man.' I wonder what he's driving at with that statement?*

"Well, since you put it that way, how dare I to refuse?"

"What time would you like to leave?" Anthony asked.

"Whatever time is good for you. It's your money, so it's your decision."

"I like the way you think." He smiled. "I like to eat lunch late. That way, it makes the rest of the day seem to go by much faster. Shall we say two o'clock?"

"Dag, when you say 'late' you really mean late. Well, if it's 2p.m. you want, then 2p.m. is what you're going to have."

He smiled wider this time. "I just love the way you think."

They walked to the mall together. It was next door. She followed as he showed her the quick way to get there. The name of the eatery he'd chosen, which he said was his favorite, was The Cajun Grille. He ordered the Bourbon Chicken special and suggested that she order the same. He told her it was his favorite place, so she trusted his judgment of the food. He ordered Bourbon Chicken for her as well.

They sat down at the table that he chose. He noticed that she blessed her food before she began to eat but he said nothing about it.

"So, Evette, how do like working for Crime Prevention?"

"It's a job." She said. "It's better than not working at all."

"No, really. Do you like it here?"

"Actually, I really do. Melissa told me that she's looking for someone full time and permanent and that she was going to see what she could do to get me hired on with benefits and all."

"Well, Melissa is the one that could probably do it. Trust me, if she doesn't like you, you're gone and seeing as though you've been here for six weeks now, I'd say she likes you. Did you know she and the Lt. Governor are friends?"

"No, I didn't and how do you know I've been here for approximately six weeks now? Are you clocking my time or something?" She lifted her right eyebrow a tad bit.

"Well, like I said, my cubicle is just a few feet away from yours."

"But," she added, "that has nothing to do with you clocking my time."

He changed the subject. "I also noticed that you like to read. Who is your favorite author?"

This man has really been checking me out. Well, he's got another thing coming if he thinks something is going to come out of this. "I'm into Sidney Sheldon right now. I think I might have read half of his collection thus far."

"Which one is your favorite one and why?"

"Well, I would say 'A Stranger in the Mirror' because it shows the reality of show business and how not every beautiful young girl that goes to Hollywood actually makes it. Most of the time they don't and to survive, they sometimes end up doing things that they otherwise wouldn't choose to do."

"So you like books based upon reality?"

"No, my taste in books is the same as my taste in music. I like versions of them all, some more than others, but versions of them all."

"You are a very interesting woman, Evette. I'm sure your husband feels very lucky to have you."

Bingo, there it is. He wants to see what life is like at home so he can see if he stands a chance at getting some. "As a matter of fact, yes he does know how *blessed* he is to have a woman like me."

"Well," he looked at his watch, "It's about time for us to be heading back. Tomorrow.."

She cut him off. "What do you mean, tomorrow?"

"Tomorrow, we'll continue our conversation over lunch and you can ask me anything you want to know about me." He stood and waited for her to do the same. *This brother has some kind of nerves assuming that because I ate with him today that I'll eat with him tomorrow.* They laughed and talked all the way back to the office and by the time they reached their cubicles, they both knew in their hearts that tomorrow would be a repeat of today. It had been a long time since she'd actually enjoyed the conversation of a man. Alexander was quiet and didn't like to talk, except for moaning during sex.

Evette got off work at 4:30p.m. and it took her two and a half hours to get home on the buses, and by the time she arrived, it was all she could do to cook dinner. When dinner was finished, they assisted A.J. with his homework. Alexander would watch television and she'd either read a book or talk on the phone to one of the sisters from the church. The kids always watched television with their daddy. Then he would give them their baths and everyone would go to bed. The most they talked was during sex or when she was fussing at him about something. The longer they were together, the further they drifted apart. It was a distance that anyone could see.

The next day, as they headed out the door, they discovered that their car was gone. A.J. got upset. "Mommy, some bad man stole our car." He said, and he started to cry. Evette went back in the house and called Crime Prevention to let them know that she would be late.

"I don't believe this mess!" She frustratingly exclaimed.

"Baby, don't worry. Everything will be fine." Alexander tried to console her, but it wasn't working. "Look, I'll stay home with the children today and you go on to work."

"I'll call you after I find out what is going on with the car." She said.

It was mid-October, so it was starting to get cold. She walked to the bus stop, knowing that it was going to take her a good two hours to get to Towson. She was totally pissed off. *I don't understand what's happening. First the house, now the car. Everything is falling apart.*

At the house, Alexander was thinking to himself as well. *Well, at least now we can start over. This time, things will be in MY name and not hers. I guess she thinks she's super woman or something. Well, let's see her get out of this. I have already filed chapter 7, so I have nothing to worry about. Serves her right.*

By the time Evette arrived at Crime Prevention it was 11a.m. and she was noticeably distraught.

"Evette, are you okay?" Tad questioned. She nodded her head. "I got your message about your car. Are you sure you're all right?"

"I'll be fine." She went to her cubicle and called the police. She couldn't believe what she was hearing. "Are you sure about that, officer?"

"Yes, ma'am. I'm sure. Your car is listed as a repo."

She hung up the phone and quickly called the Chrysler Company. "Hello. Yes, I'm Evette Worthington and I'm calling because of my car."

"Yes, it was repossessed this morning at 2a.m. for non-payment." The service rep said.

"I don't understand. I know I was two months behind but I was going to have that paid up by next week. I don't understand what happened."

"Mrs. Worthington, you are more than two months behind." She stated.

"What? That's not possible. How can that be?" She questioned.

"Mrs. Worthington, we haven't received a payment from you since June. You were four months behind."

"That's not possible. I personally gave my husband the money for July and August's payments and he sent them by quick collect."

"Well, our records show that June was the last time anything was credited to this account. You might wanna have a talk with your husband because he didn't pay it. I'm sorry Mrs. Worthington, but to get it back now, you would have to pay the towing and hold fee, and the four months of payments that are due."

"But I don't have that kind of money." She exclaimed.

"I'm sorry. But there's nothing more that we can do." She hung up.

Evette sat there and began to cry. *That dirty bastard! What did he do with my money!* She felt the left side of her face tighten, and she began to take deep breaths. The last thing she needed was to have another mild stroke. She picked up the phone and began to dial their home number, but she changed her mind. *It's been seven years of this crap. If he hasn't changed by now, chances are he never will. I'm tired of talking.*

"Evette, are you all right?" She was startled by his voice. It was Anthony. Should she lie? No, his beautiful, brown eyes would be able to see straight through it. She could always smile and say, '*I'm blessed.*' That's a phrase that most church folk hide behind. Instead, she shrugged her shoulders, dropped her eyes and said, "No, but I will be."

He stood there gazing into her eyes for a few moments. *I wish she would open up to me. It is so obvious that things are not well with her and her husband. She looks like she could stand to be held, and I would love to take her in my arms and squeeze her close to my heart. She's so fragile, yet she tries so hard to be strong.* "Well, if you should need to talk, I'm here for you."

"I won't. Don't worry." She replied.

He walked back to his cubicle and sat down at the computer. 'You've got an e-mail.' The sound came from her computer. She looked up at her screen and saw that it was from Anthony. She looked over at him and he was sitting there with his legs crossed, leaning on his desk and smiling at her. Evette couldn't believe how good he looked in his sharp creased, khaki L.L. Bean pants and his white Oxford shirt. She shook her head and rolled her eyes. It was as if she was telling him, *You just don't give up, do you?* She took a deep breath, let it out slowly and opened the e-mail.

It is obvious that something is going on with you. I hope it only serves to increase your appetite. After all, we are scheduled to have lunch together today and it is your turn to ask me questions. Seeing as though I have taken the time to prepare an answer for any possible question you may have, I would be very disappointed if my night-long efforts were in vain. I will be at your desk to pick you up at 2p.m. Don't even think you can get out of this. I know where you work. ☺

When she finished reading his e-mail, she shook her head, looked at him, smiled and turned to type a response. 'You've got an e-mail.' He turned to his computer screen to read the thoughts of her heart.

You are the most arrogant man I have ever met. Seeing as though it is so obvious that something is going on with me, what makes you think I would want to spend my lunch hour staring into your face? I do not believe that you spent your night thinking up answers to any question I might ask. I guess you must need a life.

This time, he looked over and she was staring at him with a smug look on her face. He mouthed the word *OUCH!* and began to type.

It appears that someone is displacing a little anger, but that's okay. We can talk about it over lunch at 2p.m. I will pick you up at your cubicle.

She couldn't believe it. *You just don't give up, do you? I don't want to talk to you about my private life. As a matter of fact, I think I'm going to lunch right now.* She hit 'send,' got up, grabbed her purse and walked away.

Anthony's mouth dropped as Evette got up and walked down the isle. He sent her a response any way. *I see that you are very strong willed. I like that in a woman and I do not feel threatened by it. I will see you later.* He returned to processing the grants for fiscal.

Evette went downstairs to the deli and purchased a pack of Saltine crackers and 50 cents worth of the cheapest bologna they had. She took a seat at a corner table for two and sat with her back facing the window. Her kind of misery did not enjoy company. She bowed her head and silently blessed her food as if it was a full course meal.

"Is this seat taken?" It was a familiar voice. The one she'd walked away from. She slowly lifted her head to see Anthony standing there. *God, he is so fine!* She thought.

"Actually, yes it is." She answered. He sat down anyway. "Look," she continued. "I really would like to be alone right now. Okay?" Imitating a line from *Rush Hour*, one of her favorite movies, she said, "Do you understand the words that are coming out of my mouth?" And they both burst into laughter.

"You don't have to sit here like this. Let me take you to lunch." He requested.

Evette looked down at the two slices of bologna, wrapped them up and placed them and the crackers in her purse. Looking up at him, she said. "You are like a slow steady drip on a rock."

"Huh?" *He obviously didn't know that I was referencing a scripture from the Bible.*

"Never mind." She said.

He extended his hand. "After you." *I bet she thinks I don't know that's in the Bible.*

They walked to *The Cajun Grille* at Towson Town Center mall. Once again, he ordered the Bourbon Chicken for the two of them, paid for the meal, and picked a table for them to be seated at.

"Well, I do believe it's your turn." He said.

"What? My turn for what?" She asked.

"It's your turn to ask me what ever you like."

His mouth dropped open and he stared at her as she lifted some chicken to her mouth. Her eyes were closed, so she didn't see him entranced by the moment. She closed her lips around the fork, licked her lips and lifted her head. *I bet her tongue can work wonders.*

"Okay. First question. What brought you to America?" She asked

"I'm here on a student visa. Next question."

"How long have you been here and what is your major?"

"I have been here for two years and I am majoring in Information Technology. I will be graduating next December."

"What? You've been in this Country for two years and you'll be graduating next December? Do you know it takes the average American five years to finish a four-year major? And that's if they go full time."

"Yeah, I know. That's because you Americans are spoiled and lazy."

"Watch it now. Don't get jacked-up." She lifted her fists.

He smiled. "You're cute." He said, but she pretended not to hear. "What else would you like to know about me?"

"Tell me about yourself, your family, and Africa."

"Well, Africa is a very large continent. Why don't I just narrow it down to my home, Nigeria? Nigeria is a very poor, but beautiful place. The people there are very close, like a family."

"You mean that 'it takes a village' thing is true?" She interrupted.

"Yes. But like everything else, people are separated by boundaries. I never saw a poor person until I was a junior in what you all would call 'High School.' Man," his face lit up, "we would work so hard in school. They had us writing all the time about everything. They told us that writing was an important skill to have in America."

"What about your family? Are you an only child?" She asked.

"Why, do I seem spoiled to you?"

"Actually, yes. You seem accustomed to getting what you want."

"If you pursue something hard enough, eventually, you will get it, especially women."

She ignored him again.

He continued. "I am spoiled but I am not an only child. I am the oldest of four children. My father and mother somehow managed to spoil all of us equally." His smiled broadened as he thought of his parents. "They loved us so much. My mother stayed home with us but we had a nanny that took care of the menial things."

"You had a nanny?" She asked.

"Yes. My father took very good care of us. My mother has never worked a day of their marriage." He paused and asked, "You know what I want?"

"What's that?" Evette wondered.

"I want to be at least half the man that my father is." Anthony said.

"He sounds like a very strong, hardworking, family man."

"That indeed he is. And when he would come home from a business trip, he always brought everyone something back. He truly spoiled us."

"I noticed that you like to read, too. Who's your favorite author and why?" She asked.

"It appears that I am not the only one who is doing some watching." He lifted his eyebrows at here. "I like Stephen King."

"Stephen King? Now that is a surprise. Why Stephen?"

"Are you kidding? Have you ever read any of his books?" He asked.

"Actually, no. I've seen some of his movies; *Pet Cemetery*, Carrie, etc. I figured if his movies are that demented, then the books are worse. I think Stephen King has some major issues."

"You should read some of his books before you pass judgment. He really is an excellent author." He glanced at his watch. "It's time to head back." He held her chair. "I really enjoy talking with you. It's refreshing to find a woman who is not afraid to intelligently speak her mind."

"Are you always so full of crap or is this just how you really are?" She smiled.

"You know, Evette, you are a lot smarter than you give yourself credit for and the next time you are given a compliment, you should just say 'thank you.' Trust me, you are worthy of it. I will take you home after work."

She paused and looked at him. "Oh, you will, will you? And where did you get that idea? I didn't ask you for a ride home." She was a bit perturbed.

"That's because you are too proud to ask someone to help you. You'd rather suffer in silence hoping that some day things will get better. And there's nothing wrong with that, but sometimes you need to accept the kindness of a stranger. After all, you never who cares about what you're going through." He grabbed her arm and for a moment their eyes locked and time stood still.

"You're right." She broke the suspension. "We do need to get back."

Shortly after they returned to the office, Anthony came to her cubicle.

"Taste this and tell me what you think." It was a mango. She'd had one before, but she appeased him and took a bite.

"It's delicious. Thank you." She said.

"You're very welcome." He replied and then returned to his seat.

When 4:30 arrived, she quietly left and took the bus home.

Does she actually think I didn't notice her leaving? I wish I could have a chance to make her happy. I would be so very good both to and for her.

Before she knew it, it was the end of November and they had less than a week to get out of the house before the sheriff would come and put them out. Although she believed God would work things out, she was becoming frustrated with the fact that He seemed to have a habit of waiting until the last possible minute and then allowing things to fall smoothly in line. She figured that God just liked to do that so He alone could get the glory. Which is kool. He's God, so He can do that.

"Baby, the Lord is going to work it out. You'll see." Alexander told her as they packed their belongings in the last boxes.

"He wouldn't have to work it out if you'd gotten off your lazy butt, handled your business and worked to pay your bills." She snapped.

"Baby, I just believe that God has something better for us, that's all. Don't you believe it?" He said.

"Alexander, I really think you should get out of my facc right now." She responded.

"You don't mean that." He replied.

She threw up her hands. "You know what? Since you won't leave me alone, why don't I leave you alone?" She left the living room and stormed upstairs into the bedroom. She fell across the bed, hit the pillow and began to cry.

At that moment, the phone rang. It was the manager of the last apartment she had applied for and it was on the other side of Baltimore.

"Hello, may I speak with Ms. Evette Worthington."

"Speaking." She said.

"This is Mr. Holloway from Black Pelican Apartments. I just wanted to let you know that you have the apartment."

"We, what? What?" She wanted to be sure she'd heard him correctly.

"I said you have the apartment. All we need is your deposit and first month's rent and you can move in at your convenience."

"You mean we don't have to pay a double deposit plus first and last month's rent?" She couldn't believe it.

"No. We are aware of the flipping scandal that has rocked Maryland, in particularly Baltimore City. When you came in the office, you seemed like a nice Christian woman and I talked the owner into giving you a chance. So, how soon can you have the money in here?"

"Will Saturday be okay?" She asked.

"That's perfect. I'll give you your key then."

She hung up the phone and turned to see Alexander standing in the doorway smiling. Before he could say anything, she said, "Okay, okay, okay. You told me so."

That Friday she had an appointment with Social Services. They only had half the money and they were told that they could get the remaining balance from there. Her boss had one of the coworkers to take her there. She felt embarrassed that this white man was taking her, a black woman, all the way across town to the Department of Social Services to pick up government money for assistance in moving into an apartment. *It's funny*, she thought, *there are no programs to help you save your home, but they will give you money to relocate. That just doesn't make any sense to me at all.*

When they returned to the office, she thanked Tad and her boss for allowing her to go and take care of things. She didn't say much to Anthony, but they did correspond a bit via e-mails about religious ideologies. At the end of the day, Anthony asked her how everything went. She assured him that things went well and that they would be moving the next morning. Everyone knew she was moving, because she had passed around fliers stating that she was having a house sale. Anthony had shown interest in her bookcase, until he found out it wasn't big enough. He was an avid reader and had more books than she did.

The next day, Alexander's father came to help them move. Evette thought that they had packed everything, but she was still finding things that had somehow been overlooked. With the first load of things placed on the van, they headed off. Thirty minutes later, they were on the other side of Baltimore; she paid the money, got the key and went to the apartment to scrub it down with bleach and Pine-Sol while their things were brought in. It took them all day and most of the night to move everything. Thus confirming that old cliché, 'you never know how much junk you have until you're ready to move.'

Around 6pm Evette heard a knock at the door. *Who could this possibly be?* She wondered. She ran down the stairs, which were inside the apartment, and opened the door. She couldn't believe her eyes. It was Melissa and two of her three daughters. In her hands she held an extra large cheese pizza and they all wore giant smiles on their faces.

"We're not going to stay." She said. "We just thought you might not feel like cooking, so we brought you dinner and some more things."

"Oh, my God, Melissa, you're a jewel." She hugged her neck and the children's as well. "Come on in." They all headed up the stairs.

"Evette, it smells so good in here." Melissa said as the scent of the Pine-Sol penetrated her nostrils.

"Thanks, we just got the keys today, so I didn't have a chance to come in before hand to clean up. Here. Let me take that." She took the pizza and set it on top of the stove. She showed Melissa around the apartment. It was a two-bedroom, so it really didn't take very long for them to see it. Evette had already put most of the decorations up, so it did have somewhat of a pleasant touch to it.

"Evette, this is wonderful! No more two hour commutes to work for you."

"Yeah, thank God!" They laughed and hugged each other.

"I have some more things in the van for you." Melissa said.

"What? Girl, you've done more than enough." Evette said.

"Well, this will keep you from having to spend money for a while." She responded.

Within minutes, Melissa and her two daughters were bringing in bags of food. Evette thanked them and then they said, "Oh, we're not nearly finished." Evette took the bags and set them in the kitchen. Each time she returned to the door, there were more bags. This happened about ten times. She wanted to cry. Everyone in the office thought that Melissa was an evil person, but she was the kindest that Evette had ever had the pleasure of working with. She had been nothing short of a blessing the moment they met each other.

By the time they finished, Evette's pantry was full, as well as her refrigerator and freezer. They'd also brought toys and games for the children for Christmas, plus paper and tape to wrap the gifts with. Melissa thought of everything. They hugged and kissed each other on the cheeks and Melissa and the kids were on their way. Two weeks later, Dora did the same thing, food and Christmas gifts for the children. Evette had so much food, she found herself giving bags of it away to another family that had children. And when Monday arrived, Melissa had two bags of clothes for Evette.

"Hey, congratulations on your new home." It was Anthony. He was standing behind her. She turned to respond but found herself almost speechless. She cleared her throat.

"Yeah, God blessed us in the nick of time." She said.

"Yeah, right. Anyway, can I treat you to lunch today? Just to celebrate."

"I don't know about that." Evette said. "Maybe another time.

"All right. Another time." He walked back to his desk and sat done. Moments later, she heard, 'you've got an e-mail' on her computer. It was from him. She looked over at him, he was looking at her and smiling, and she mouthed 'you just left from over here.'

He mouthed back, 'just read it.'

"What?" She mouthed again.

"Read it." He said slowly and pointed to the screen.

She opened the e-mail and it was something he'd written in his native language. As she got ready to turn toward him again, he was standing behind her.

"It means 'don't fight' in my language." He said.

"How do you pronounce it?" She asked.

"It's pronounced 'my ja-aw.' And like I said, it means don't fight."

"Don't fight what?" She inquired.

"Don't fight anything." Anthony said.

The buzzer on Evette's phone rang. "Evette?" It was Melissa. "Can you come to my office please, and bring a pad and pen with you." "I'm on my way." She answered. Turning to look at Anthony, "Well, I gotta go. I'll talk to you later."

"You will?" He inquired.

"Yes. I will." She said.

Melissa's office was on the other side of the hall where the Executive Director's office was. It was like entering into the twilight. On the side where she sat, everyone was casual and laid back. Sure they had their pressures as far as deadlines and grant monitoring but overall it was like one big family. The other side, however, was like entering into the king's palace. It was an obvious difference there. The people were much more uptight, hardly anyone was cordial and then there was the Executive Director who seemed to have a need for feeling important - though he was an important man, he just wasn't humble. When you were in his presence, he made it quit obvious if he thought anything of you or not.

She knocked on the door. "Come in Evette." Melissa said.

"Good morning Melissa. Before we begin, I just wanted to thank you again for what you and your family did for us when we moved into the new apartment."

"Oh, don't even think about it." Melissa said. "If we say that we're Christians and believers, we should show it. Showing love to our neighbors is the least we can do. Don't you agree?"

"Yes, I do." She said.

"Now, to the business at hand. I want you to type a memo for me." She proceeded to give her the details for the memo. "Also, I need you to coordinate a meeting with Daniel. I don't know why it's so hard for me to get on his calendar? Anyway, there is one more thing. I'm really trying my best to get you hired on here with benefits. I just need you to continue working hard and doing your best, like you've always done. I think it would be easier for you to shine if you worked with the Communications Team full time instead of being divided between this and the Program Committee. But that's my battle. You just sit quietly and let me see what I can work out for you."

They shook hands. "Thank you, Melissa."

"No problem. Now run along and get that memo typed for me." They smiled at each other as Evette gently closed the door behind her. Evette rushed back across the hall, typed the memo and distributed it. The next two weeks were pretty intense especially with the Christmas holiday approaching. Everyone wanted to wrap up all of their projects and all of their site visits but people were constantly taking time off and going shopping. It was a good thing that Evette was such a hyperactive person otherwise she wouldn't have been able to keep up.

"I have something for you. Can I take you to lunch to give it to you?" Anthony asked.

"Sure, I'd love to eat lunch with you today, but today, I am paying for my own food." She smiled. She was glad that their finances finally afforded her the opportunity to purchase her own lunch for a change.

They went to County Town Center mall and Anthony ordered the Bourbon Chicken special. She chose something different this time, fried rice, beef and broccoli, and noodles. As usual, she let him pick the table.

"So, what is this surprise that you have?" Evette inquired.

"I did not say that it was a surprise." He answered.

"What is it? Where is it?" She asked.

"Calm down and eat your lunch. It's here but not with me." Anthony said.

"What? You're full of it." She said.

"Let's just eat lunch and enjoy the ambiance of the holiday."

"Okay." She said, as she took a big bite of broccoli. While chewing it, she said, "So, tell me more about Africa."

"I told you, Africa is a pretty big continent." He said.

"Okay. Nigeria. Tell me more about Nigeria." She continued to eat her food.

"You're going to choke if you don't slow down. You eat much too fast. You should enjoy your food. It should be more than just satisfying your hunger. It should be an experience." He said.

"I see you've rented 'Soul Food' over the weekend." They laughed. "Now, tell me more about Nigeria."

"Well, there's not much left to tell." He said.

"No, now, the last time we spoke, you talked mostly about yourself, your family and your upbringing. I know your mother is an awesome woman; your father is dedicated and hardworking and spoiled the crap out of all four of his kids. You didn't see a poor person until you were almost finished with high school and you and your buddies worked out using a make shift gym that you created with old car parts. Now, tell me about Nigeria." She smiled.

"Well, as you are aware, Nigeria is a very poor country. It's beautiful, though. Because it's so poor, it survives by trafficking drugs to countries like the United States. There really isn't much more to tell." He stopped to eat more food.

"What? Are you telling me the truth? What about this big 'war on drugs' campaign that America has been so fierce about?" Evette asked.

"Yes, that's how most poor countries get money. They will never get rid of drugs, especially in the United States. There are too many people making money. They will continue to pound the people on the lower rung of the ladder but as far as any major things happening that would really bring about a change, forget about it. There's too much money out there." Anthony answered.

"So then, America is the Kingpin of the world. I guess Baltimore City would be its capitol, especially with the heroine problem we have." She said.

They continued to talk about family, kids, and the roles of a husband and a wife. When they finished eating, they went to a bookstore.

"I noticed that you love to read." He said as he walked swiftly down one particular isle. He knew exactly what he was there for and didn't take time to browse around like Evette was trying to do.

"Can you slow down a bit? I'm trying to check out the shelves." She said as she tried to catch up with him. "And are you still watching me? How do you know I like to read?"

"Every time you have a chance, your head is in a book. Everyone knows that you love to read. It's not like you try to hide it. When you eat lunch at your desk, you almost always have a book in your hands." He paused. He'd reached the area he wanted to be at. "Who's your favorite author?" He asked.

"I told you before, lately I've been engrossed with Sidney Sheldon." She answered.

"Sidney Sheldon? I think he's mediocre." He said.

"All right. Leave Sidney alone." She warned. "I think he's a gifted writer. He can go from writing love stories, to political stories, to science fiction and still not lose the ability to capture your imagination and leave you in suspense."

"Have you ever read anything by Jeffrey Archer?" He asked.

"I never heard of him." She stated.

"Then you're not as into reading as I thought you were." There was a whole wall in the bookstore filled with Jeffrey Archer's books. Anthony found the two that he wanted and handed them to Evette. "Merry Christmas." He said. "Read this one first." It was entitled 'Cain and Able.' "Then read this one." It was 'The Prodigal Daughter.' Then he reached into his coat pocket and pulled out a video tape. "I didn't have time to have it wrapped." He looked away for a moment and then turned to look her in the eyes.

"What's this?" Evette asked. "An exercise tape! Are you trying to be smart or something?"

"No, its just that I overheard you and another temp talking about losing weight after the holidays and I just thought that since you said you are allergic to exercise, this eight minute Tae-Bo workout tape would be just the thing you needed to get you started."

She smiled and gave him a hug. "Thank you, Anthony. I appreciate this. I really do." They headed back to the office.

"You guys are late." The receptionist said. "Every one has been looking for you. Where were you guys?"

"We were eating lunch." Evette said. "And we weren't gone that long.

"You've been gone an hour and a half, to be exact." She said. "You're half an hour late getting back. Are you two trying to start seeing each other or something?" She inquired.

"Girl, please. I'm a married woman, and besides Anthony and I are just friends. Or don't you think it's possible for blacks to be 'just friends?'" Evette said, with an attitude. She was offended.

"I'll talk to you later." Anthony said as he left.

Time seemed to fly by swiftly and before she knew it, Christmas had come and gone. The church had sponsored them for the holidays. So members from the Hospitality Committee brought them food, gifts and an artificial Christmas tree with all the trimmings. When January came, the entire office was in training classes that were being held in a hotel in Towson. The classes were fun and informative and the food was incredibly delicious.

Dora had given Melissa a wonderful idea about starting a Crime Prevention newsletter for all of their constituents and at that point they'd had about three issues produced. Dora had done all of the work herself. That day, she came and sat with Anthony and Evette during the training's lunch break because she wanted to interview Anthony as the featured employee of the month. They were polite, but by this time they really began to look forward to the time that they spent alone. When the issue came out, Evette found herself cutting Anthony's picture out and putting it in her wallet behind her driver's license.

By now, she'd lost a lot of weight. She had gone from one hundred eighty eight pounds to one hundred forty nine and everyone was starting to notice, including Anthony. Her husband was complementing her as well, but by now, she was so disgusted with having lost their home, their car and him filing chapter 7 bankruptcy and leaving her with close to eighty thousand dollars worth of debt, she began sleeping on the couch. She didn't even want to have sex with him. It seemed as if all desire had fled to some distant place and even when she tried to force herself to think about it, the thought or sight of him would turn her cold.

On Valentine's Day, Alexander had bought her several balloons, a card, and some candy. She appreciated it, but was upset that he'd used some of the bill money to do it. More than anything, she wanted to get out of debt. She'd already gone behind his back and purchased twenty-five shares of stock in a banking company, now she was thinking of a plan to leave him and the church. They were both licensed ministers, but she'd lost her passion for ministry. She'd been through so much until she just got tired. She wasn't sure if it was worth it anymore. At work, she gave Anthony a Hershey's chocolate kiss and seeing him smile really made her day.

Two weeks later, when they were scheduled to look at the car that he wanted to give her, but she insisted on purchasing from him, she and Alexander got into an argument. In the middle of the argument, Anthony called. She answered the phone and he asked to speak to the person who makes the decisions. Though he was just joking, it wasn't the right time for it, but he had no way of knowing that.

Anthony made arrangements with Alexander to pick him and the children up to take them to see the car. Evette was not going with them, thus the reason for the argument. She had been invited as a guest to a luncheon that was being hosted by the sister organization to the NAACP. The person who had invited her had already paid for the ticket so she couldn't get out of it.

Her ride picked her up before Anthony arrived to pick up Alexander and the kids. The banquet went very well. The food was good and the ladies were nice and friendly. By the time it was over, she and the woman she rode with ran two errands during which time Evette asked the older woman to pray for her. She was about to get out of her marriage.

The woman told her how she had been married for years and had twelve children. She struggled through issues of domestic violence and the church. Her husband was a deacon who beat her severely and molested all of their daughters. Eventually, she realized that she had to get out, so she left him and the church, too and never returned to either again. She spoke with much pain in her voice, as she blamed the church for not being there to help her while she was going through. She felt as if they blamed her and protected him because they taught that if your husband beat you, it was because you weren't humble or obedient enough. Or, if you were being humble and obedient, then God must be trying to teach you some deeper lesson or else it wouldn't be happening. After her experience, she said she began to admonish women that it's better to get out than to stay in and lose yourself in the process.

When Evette finally arrived home, everyone was asleep and had been since 1pm. She was totally pissed off because that meant that since the children were now waking up at 6pm, they wouldn't be ready to go to bed at their scheduled time which was 9 O'clock. Alexander had, once again, gotten her back in his passive aggressive way. Also, she found a disconnection notice that he'd tried to hide. She discovered that he had not paid the gas and electric bill for three months. She called the company and asked when the last payment was made. Though she had separated the money for the bills, he had not paid them. She confronted him.

"Alexander, did you pay the gas and electric bill this month?" She asked, as nicely as possible.

"Yeah. Why?" He answered.

"What about last month?" She kept going.

"Yes. I paid all of the bills." He insisted.

"Then why did we get a cut off notice in the mail today?" She held the bill up in front of his face.

"I think they just got something messed up in their system." He lied.

"I called them Alexander. The last payment they received was the one that I paid three months ago." She shook her head. "Are you on drugs or something?"

"What are you talking about? No, I'm not on any drugs." He became defensive.

"Then are you seeing someone else? Are you giving your money to some woman instead of paying your bills and taking care of your children, because I haven't asked you for a damn thing since I was pregnant with A.J. six and a half years ago!" She shouted.

"Now, that's enough! You will not use that type of language when you're talking to me! You need to repent!"

"You know what? You're right. I do need to repent. I repent that I ever met you. I repent that I took off work for the week of the convention because had I been at work, I never would have met you. I repent that I even married you in the first place. No good thing has come out of this relationship outside of our two children." She threw her hands up.

"Evette, you need to calm down, repent and pray." He began to walk away. "I have to get ready to go to work."

She stood there and began to cry. After they had lost everything, then he decided to get a part time job at IHOP. She asked God to forgive her for cussing. By now, the children were up and wired. They were running around playing and laughing with no hope of going to bed any time soon, while she, on the other hand, was ready to crawl under the bed and go to sleep.

The week before, on Sunday night, Anthony had come over for dinner and to talk to Alexander about buying the car. It was Alexander's idea. Anthony had brought a bottle of White Zinfandel wine, not knowing that it was her favorite. She grabbed it from the refrigerator, went into the bedroom, closed the door and proceeded to get drunk.

For some reason she began to think about the dreams she'd been having lately and how strange they'd been. For about six weeks straight, she'd dreamed of Anthony. Nothing sexual, just him, standing in the distance surrounded by darkness, calling her. "Evette. Evette. Come to me, Evette. Evette, come to me." Each night it was the same thing until on the last night, it was as if he was right in her face, "I got you!" And she woke up trembling. She didn't try to figure out what the dreams meant and maybe she just didn't want to know.

She picked up the phone and dialed his number. His phone rang.

"Hello," the answer came in a thick Nigerian accent. "Hi."

"Evette? Is that you?"

"Yeah."

"What's wrong?"

"I called to apologize to you for my behavior today on the phone. I'm sorry. You didn't deserve that. We were in the middle of an argument when you called and...well, I'm sorry."

"You have nothing to apologize for. I wasn't offended. Anyway, I was just kidding with what I said." There was a pause. "Are you crying?"

"Yes."

"You sound funny. What are you doing?"

"I'm getting drunk off the wine you brought on Sunday for dinner."

"Why are you crying and getting drunk? Where are your husband and your children?"

"Alexander is at work. The kids are playing and are about to go to bed."

"So why are you hurting yourself?"

"Because I'm tired."

"Tired of what?"

"Everything." She broke down. The tears began to pour like streams of water from a broken dam, and she opened herself up to him. "I'm tired of being neglected. I'm tired of being unappreciated and taken for granted. I'm tired of being the main source of income for this family..."

He interrupted. "I didn't know things were that bad. I was under the impression that you and your husband had the ideal marriage."

"You were able to think that only because I'm a good actress and I've grown accustomed to wearing a mask in public."

"Do you wanna talk about it?"

"Not with you."

"Why?"

"Because I'm a Christian and you're an atheist. That's why."

"Like I told you at work, an atheist is the best person for a Christian to talk to because you don't have to worry about information that's one-sided, nor do you have to worry about being indoctrinated. All I could do is offer you a fresh perspective."

"Well, alright. It started when we were first married. The first 2-½ months were bliss. Then one of his brothers came to our home, beat me and tried to rape me. Things have been down hill since then because I haven't been able to let it go. I mean, he didn't do *anything*. I would have at least felt better if he'd yelled at him, but he didn't even do that."

She continued. "Last year, we lost our house, our car. He filed bankruptcy, now I have no choice but to do it too before they come after me. My family is so disgusted until they told me they won't do another thing to help me unless I leave him and take the children with me."

He quietly listened as she went on about how her father owns his own company in Nevada and promised to buy her a house out there and said she could work for the company. Her aunt in Maine promised her a job as Assistant Manager of one of the apartment complexes that she over sees and told her she could live there rent-free. Martha told her that the last things she'd ever have to worry about are where she's going to live and work. All she had to do was leave her husband.

He sighed. "My heart goes out for you. If you would please forgive me for saying this, but your husband is a moron."

"If he's a moron, what does that make me? After all, I did marry him."

"That makes you human." He heard her sigh. "Are you alright? How much have you consumed so far?"
"Almost the entire bottle. I'm feeling pretty mellowed out right about now."

"Can I ask you a question?"

"Sure, anything you like. Doesn't mean I have to answer it, though."

"What is it that you want from your husband?"

She took a deep breath and let it out slowly. "I want him to appreciate me and the things I do. I want him to make me feel special." She began to cry a bit. "I want him to make love to me. To take his time and make love to me. Make me into a sundae. Put whip cream all over me and take his time licking and sucking it off. I want him to savor me. To talk to me sometimes. He can start there."

"I wish I was there to hold you right now."

She was startled by his confession but since he was being open, she decided to do so as well. "To be honest with you, I wish you were here to hold me, too."

"You lie."

"No. I've been attracted to you for months. I've been dreaming about you for weeks now, every night."

This time she heard him sigh. "What are you doing?"

He ignored her question. "Can you do me a favor?" he asked.

"Sure. Anything."

"Can you caress yourself for me?"

She did and sighed. She couldn't believe how wet she was just from hearing the
sound of his voice.

"Now, stick your fingers inside you."

She did, and sighed again. Then she sucked her juices from her fingers. He heard the sound and asked, "What was that?"

She said, "Oh, I just tasted myself, that's all."

He sighed heavily. "How do you taste?"

"Sweet."

Another heavy sigh and he said, "I'll be there in ten minutes."

"Are you crazy? There is no way I'm going to let you come in here and screw me in my husband's bed with my kids here. No way."

He suggested his car. She told him she wasn't some high school girl or college freshman.

"Is it because you're drunk?"

"No. I believe people use alcohol and drugs as scapegoats for having said or done what they always wanted to. I've never been so drunk that I did or said anything unwittingly. If I say it or do it, it's because I always wanted to. I think people should stop blaming their behavior on substances. If I screw you at all, it will be because I've wanted to for a while anyway, not because I'm inebriated. O.K.?"

"What are your children doing now?"

"They are asleep."

"Can I come?"

"No."

"Please. I want you so badly. I want to hold you, to feel you, to comfort you. I've desired you for a while also. You're so beautiful and your eyes, they're just exquisite. I'm so hard. Can I come?"

"Yes."

He was shocked. "You won't change your mind when I get there will you?"

"No."

"Promise?"

"I promise."

"I'll be there in ten minutes."

"I'll be waiting outside."

As drunk as she was, she ran into the bathroom, plugged in the curlers and hopped in the shower. Then she bumped a few curls in her hair, brushed her teeth, put Elizabeth Arden's *Splendor* scented lotion all over her body and hopped in a silk negligee. She threw on a long, black trench coat, got the White Zinfandel wine bottle and waited for him outside. The children were in their beds knocked out for the night. She saw the lights of his burgundy Camaro turn into the parking lot and smiled.

He met her half way and when they were face-to-face, he grabbed her waist, pulled her to him and stuck his tongue in her mouth. She responded and they were off. She'd almost slipped getting into the car, but his strength bore her up. When they began to drive off, they glanced at each other with anticipation and smiled. He stuck his fingers up her vagina and she rotated her hips with pleasure. Then he sucked her juices from his fingers and caressed her cheek with his hand. He grasped her left hand and placed it on his penis. He was as hard as a rock, and in her mind, he seemed to have a length that went on forever.

Within minutes they were at his place. It was your typical Baltimore brownstone. He told her that one of his cousins owned it and rented it out to members of the family. He lived on the third floor, a female cousin lived on the second floor and another cousin and his wife and kids lived on the first floor. He turned the alarm off and they quietly tipped up the stairs. He'd left the television on BET and all the lights were off – only the television lit the room.

He took the wine from her and sat it on the table. Then he turned and stared her in the eyes. For a few moments, they were suspended in time. He unzipped her coat and smiled as he saw what she was wearing; a whit, silk negligee with wine colored flowers trimmed in gold. "Nice." He said and then proceeded to quickly remove it.

He held her so tightly and kissed her so passionately. It was almost as if he was trying to ravish her. She felt, for the first time in a long time, safe, secure, wanted, protected. His tongue was so sweet and he was hungry with a passion she'd not seen since college.

He picked her up and she wrapped her legs around his back as he lowered her onto the floor. She was impressed with his strength. His body was so hard and muscular, like a finely chiseled work of art made by an ancient Greek sculptor. They kissed wildly, passionately, and then suddenly, gently, sensuously. He moved slowly downward caressing her body with his lips, massaging her with his tongue, until he reached her vagina. He had already told her on the phone about his sexual version of the ABC's and how no woman had ever made it to Z. Her response to him was that she could probably go through it three or four times and still not climax. At that, they began to view one another as a worthy challenge.

True enough, his tongue performed an alphabetical symphony on her clitoris. He literally traced every single letter. But before she could climax, and it was after several choruses, he got up, kissed her, smiled and said, "Not yet." When he placed his tongue in her mouth, she grabbed it and began to suck it the way she would suck his penis. From the way he reacted, she doubted if anyone had ever kissed him that way before. Then she began to guide him upward. He quickly caught the message. He placed his penis over her face and she gasped. It was so big and so long that she almost chickened out in fear!

She began to make love to his penis. It was so unique. In her hands it felt like silk and it was as smooth as melted chocolate in her mouth. She began to suck and lick and nibble his balls and he was like a puppy running frenzily to his new master. He could barely handle it. He snatched her up, carried her into his bedroom and closed the door. Despite the fact that she was extremely self-conscience about her out of shape body, he wanted the lights on. Later, he told her that he can tell when a woman climaxes; her pupils dilate. He wanted to see her pupils to make sure he knew she wasn't faking.

He began to suck and lick her vagina again. He actually made love to her and she to him in every position imaginable and then in some even she'd never heard of before. And the things he said! He'd pulled her on top of him and began to suck her very worn breasts. Being self-conscience, she said, "These breasts have nursed two babies," and she dropped her head.

His response was, "Let them nurse a third." At one point, he was on top of her and the upper portion of her body was hanging somewhat off the bed. He told her, as he stared deeply into her eyes, "I count it an honor and a pleasure being with you. It feels as if we are writing a verse to the oldest form of poetry known to man." She melted with each word, each stroke of his manliness, but he would not allow her to climax just yet.

He got up and she rolled him over. She poured the warm oils she'd brought on his back and massaged him. She couldn't help but admire how his long hours of working out everyday proved beneficial to his form. When she finished, he left the room. She could hear Boys to Men's video *I'll Make Love To You* playing in the other room. He'd had her to lie on her stomach, so she didn't know he had the whip cream until she felt it on her back. Her body trembled with expectation. His tongue felt so warm and so good.

His kisses were gentle, sweet. She felt lost in his touch and calming embrace.

As he turned her over to put whip cream on her vagina, he took his time eating and licking it off. He arose briefly to kiss her. He had whip cream on his lips and she licked it off. They enjoyed savoring the sweetness of one another's tongues.

When he finally inserted himself in her, she gasped with extreme pleasure. She almost came instantly. Sensing it, he stopped, smiled down at her and said, "Not yet." This he did four times and then said; "Now it is time to conquer you." He made her say his name and by the time he finally allowed her to climax, she felt as though she'd reached the highlight of a symphony composed by the most remarkable of artists.

When it was over, they both laid there in awe. He held her in his arms as her head rested across his chest. "Evette, you have to make a decision."

And she woke up, trembling and sweating **two hours later. They had both fallen asleep in each other's arms. She looked at the alarm clock and it was one hour before Alexander was to arrive home from work. She started to wake Anthony up, but paused to take in the sight of him. Her eyes scanned his body admiringly before she gently kissed his lips and stroked his chest. She couldn't bring herself to lay her head upon his chest to listen to his heartbeat. That was a pleasure that she had reserved for one man only, Love.**

He drove her home.

"You are a dynamic woman, Evette." He said.

"You're not so bad yourself."

"So, what do you think things will be like once we return to the office on Monday?" He asked.

"Why don't we just cross that bridge when we get to it?" She replied.

He gently held her hand and stroked it with his thumb. She rested her head upon his shoulder as he drove.

Upon arriving at her apartment, she got out and he walked her to the door. As they stood there holding each other, she absorbed as much of his strength as she could. For the past five months he had become her rock, her source of encouragement and strength. In him, she found a sense of renewal.

They kissed again, sort of like a scene from a well-written romance novel and she proceeded to open the door. He jumped out of the car and ran over to her side to open it. "You have got to get re-accustomed to being treated like a lady." He said. She got out of the car, walked to her front door and stood there watching as he got into his car and drove away. Then she raced into the apartment, took a shower and put on her nightclothes. She was glad that the children had slept undisturbed while she was gone.

As she brushed her teeth, she glanced in the mirror and noticed that Anthony had put a passion mark on her neck. "Daggone it! I told him not to do that. No wonder it felt so good." She said aloud. She reached into her purse, pulled out her bottle of liquid foundation and applied a generous amount to the area. When Alexander came home, she was on the couch asleep.

Understandably why, Evette did not go to church on Sunday. She felt that the 'church world' had let her down and that there was no difference between it and the 'world.' Both were political, both had respect of persons; both were filled with greed and the vanities of life and had become shallow, empty shells of an existence long gone. She found fault with everything and everybody, but that's generally what happens when one has allowed him/herself to become spiritually defiled. You see everything through dark colored glasses because of the darkness that you have embraced into your own soul. You feel almost behooved to find, and justify the darkness that surrounds you, even if that darkness exists only within your own mind. Since the Bible says that 'to the pure, all things are pure,' it is safe then to reason that to the defiled, all things are defiled.

On Monday, there was a noticeable difference in how Anthony and Evette related to each other. In passing, they smiled at each other more, they found themselves blushing in each other's presence, and every time they had a free moment, they were talking. They found themselves doing things they hadn't done before, touching one another as they talked and using their eyes to be increasingly flirtatious.

The week seemed to swiftly pass and before they knew it, it was Friday and they were e-mailing each of with plans for the night.

"I have something special planned for you tonight." His e-mail said.

"Oh, really? What?" She responded.

"It's a surprise. I think you will enjoy it, especially since you are so uninhibited."

"Now I'm really curious. But guess what? I have a surprise for you, too."

Now his curiosity was peaking. "What is it?" He inquired.

"Since you're not telling, I'm not telling." He looked up from his cubicle to see her smiling at him. He returned the smile, and typed a response.

"I'm looking forward to experiencing you again."

After work, she walked to York Road to an adult store that she wanted to purchase some things from. She bought as black silk wrap for her shoulders, eatable, cherry flavored massage liquid, and a fury black hair band. Then she went back to the Town Center to purchase a matching set of black earrings, and a choker. She also took the bus to Harris' food market to purchase a small bag of green seedless grapes. She was set. That night, she quietly packed everything in her purse and included, as an after thought, a bottle of warmed oil.

She made sure she put the children to bed at a later time than usual to ensure that they would sleep soundly while she was away. Alexander left for work around 10:30pm and at 11:15, her phone rang.

"Hello." She answered, knowing that it was Anthony. "What's up?" Anthony asked. She loved his native accent. "I'll be there in ten minutes."

"Okay. I'll wait seven minutes and then go stand outside."

They hung up. She watched the clock, which seemed to be moving in slow motion. Finally, he showed up. He was on time, but to her, it seemed to be an eternity. She ran to the car to quickly get in, but he hopped out, ran to the passenger side and opened the door for her.

"I see you're not accustomed to being treated well by men." He said. He was right, even Alexander didn't treat her the way he did. Not that Anthony went out of the way to treat her so gentlemanly, it seemed to be a part of his character, but Alexander only did those things when someone was looking and he wanted to make an impression.

Their night was playful and wonderful. As soon as they entered his apartment, he grabbed her and pushed her on the couch.

"Oh, it's like that, huh?" She asked.

"Yeah, it's like that." He said. "I want to give you a night you will forever remember. After tonight, whenever you think of me, your body will react."

"Oh, you're that sure of yourself, huh?" She asked.

"Well, we'll see."

He went directly to her neck. First the left side. It felt indescribably good, so good, until she couldn't believe it when she felt herself begin to climax. He pressed his body hard against hers and gripped her. His left arm was wrapped around her back while his right arm went up around her shoulders as his hand held her head in place. When her quivering began to subside, he kissed her gently on the lips and cheeks as he moved to the right side of her neck.

"No, no." She whispered. But he continued. He knew that there was a spot on the right side of her neck that, when kissed, would cause her entire body to literally collapse. If there was such a thing as a 'G Spot' that was it for Evette. Sure enough, she came again and he held her and kissed her until the rippling of her body ceased.

He lifted her from the couch and escorted her into his bedroom where she began her game. She started by blind folding him and making him a 'sleeper' (a sex game that she'd learned during her freshman year at Jackson State University.) When the game was over, she proceeded to the next level.

"Do you trust me?" She asked.

"What are you planning on doing to me?" He sounded rather nervous but he put up a brave front. He'd never met a woman who was as experimental as Evette. He liked it, but at the same time, it made him nervous.

"Oh, I won't bite you. Not too hard anyway. I just want to tie you up with silk scarves, that's all." She smiled coyly.

"Okay. Go ahead." He reluctantly agreed.

She tied his wrists together and then tied his ankles together. She pulled out the bottle of oil and proceeded to give him a total body massage. He was like a finely chisled sculpture and she mounted him as if she was an Amazon Warrior. Evette pulled the seedless grapes from her purse and while he lay on his stomach, she crushed the grapes between her fingers and allowed the juice to roll across his back. After she'd crushed and eaten about ten of them, she began to lick and suck the juices from his back. To his pleasure, she began her oral symphony. Unable to stand it any longer, he began to beg her to untie him. It was truly an ego trip for her because she'd finally made this gentle giant scream.

"Please, I can't take it anymore. Evette, please untie me." He begged.

She smiled and then giggled. "Not, yet. I'm not finished."

"I will make you pay for this." He said. "Please, untie me."

After another ten minutes, she untied him. True enough, he made her pay. First, he asked to blind fold and tie her up. She was reluctant, but after a while, she consented. She lay there surrounded by darkness, trusting the fact that he wouldn't take advantage of her vulnerability. In sex, there is a tremendous difference between being tied up by a man verses being tied up by a woman. Women are playful and experimental. Men, on the other hand, have a tendency to get sadomasochistic. Fear began to grip her and her breathing became somewhat labored. Sensing it, he began to speak softly into her ears as he gently stroked her from her cheeks to her shoulders.

He kissed her as he spoke. "This is a story about a princess." He said.

"What's her name?" Evette asked, and then smiled.

"Her name is Evette. Shhhh, listen and enjoy my little tale." He continued. "This was no ordinary princess because unlike the others, she refused to marry a man without knowing whether he could satisfy her. Her appetite for sex was levels above the average woman and she did not want to live miserably through her marriage."

He continued. "One day, a handsome, chocolate skinned prince came to the castle. He was not tall in stature but he was well endowed in other areas." As he talked, he performed a medley of skillful tricks on her with his tongue, slowly moving towards her vagina.

"He presented a challenge to the princess. If he could make her cum in less than ten minutes, she would be his forever." Evette moaned with pleasure as she felt his lips caress her lips. He stuck his tongue in her mouth and she gasped. He maticulously began to place seedless grapes in her mouth and once inside, he used his middle finger to swirl them around inside her. She trembled as the walls of her body contracted around his finger. On the tenth grape, he began to suck them out and eat them.

As her body began to tremble, she begged him not to stop, but as promised, he tortured her. Five times he sensed that she was about to climax and five times he stopped. Finally, when she could no longer handle it, he licked and sucked her clit and stroked his fingers inside her until she exploded. Evette had never climaxed that hard in all her sexually active years. It was as if she was having convulsions. He locked down on her body and continued to pleasure her, even though, by now, she was begging him to stop. She had never been made to feel such ecstasy and as much as she had boasted, when it all boiled down to it, she couldn't handle it.

Finally, he inserted himself and she climaxed instantly. He put her in positions that she'd never known before. He was the most skillful lover that she'd ever been with. The way he handled her body, the way he touched and caressed her, the way he stroked her skin, and kissed her lips, he was like nothing she'd ever experienced. He was, indeed, the best.

"What's the count?" He asked as he stroked her body with his manhood.

"What?" She was snapped out of her realm of ecstasy.

"How many times have you climaxed?" Anthony inquired.

"Three." She had a hard time speaking because it felt so good.

"I think we can do better than that." He said and instantly, he took it to another level. She didn't think they could go any higher, but he proved her wrong. Anthony personified stamina, and after what seemed to be an hour, he asked,

"What's the count?"

"Five." She screamed.

"I want to give you something to think about until we meet again." He bore down on her and sensing the challenge, she began to give him all she had. He smiled at her and said, "now it is time to conquer you." He grabbed the headboard and then opened up the floodgates. Her body humbled itself to him. He was, without a doubt, the master of this game.

"What's the score?" He shouted above her screams of passion.

"Six!" She managed to somehow get it out and then something happened that had never happened to her before, her entire body went into wild convulsions, her head was spinning, the room became dark and, for a moment, she felt as if she was floating in outer space. She was snapped back into reality when she felt his body collapse on hers. They had both climaxed together.

They lay there talking as he held her tightly in his arms. Three hours later, she was awakened by what she thought was a fly. Actually, it was Anthony, playing with her nose.

"You're beautiful while you're sleeping. Did you know that?"

"Oh, so I'm ugly while I'm awake?" She laughed.

"You know what I mean." He said as he kissed her lips. "It would be very easy to wake up looking into your eyes every morning."

"You're not so bad yourself." She said, smiling.

"No. I'm not beautiful." Anthony said.

"Who lied to you?" She asked. "You're more than beautiful, you're exquisite." She reached up to touch his face with her hands. "Your eyes are so romantic, yet wise. Your nose is sexy. Your cheeks are like pillars of strength. You have a regal air about you. Why, any woman should feel honored to belong to you."

She continued. "Now, me, on the other hand. I still have about thirty five more pounds lose."

He interrupted her. "You're beautiful."

"It's after three o'clock, we'd better go." She dropped her head.

"What's the matter?" He asked.

"My marriage is crap, that's what's the matter. I wish I could combine everything about you with his spirituality. I would have the perfect man."

"As far as your troubles are concerned, just remember," He lifted her chin with his fingers, "nothing is forever." Then he caressed her stomach and said, "Not even this." He went on, "You see, weight and relationships are the same. It's about making a decision and sticking to it. Anything that is negative in your life, you can always get rid of. If you so desire."

They got dressed and left. When they pulled into the parking lot, Anthony looked her in the eyes and said, "Your husband is a very lucky man."

"Yeah, he just doesn't know it yet. That's all." She replied.

"Promise me one thing." He said.

"Anything." Evette answered.

"Promise me that you will go back to college and finish your degree." Before she could say anything, he held up a finger and said, "Even if you have to do it in spite of your husband. Do it for me, even if you don't think you can do it for yourself."

"I promise." She vowed. They kissed passionately and she got out and went inside. She took her bath, got dressed for bed and prepared the couch for bed. As soon as her head hit the pillow, the Holy Spirit began to deal with her. She could hear a still, small voice inside her.

"Come back before it's too late to return." The voice said.

"But it's already too late." She said aloud.

"It's never to late for you, Evette. God can still use you. He wants to use you. All you have to do is submit yourself to Him again. He is waiting for you to turn to Him."

"I don't have the strength to let go." She began to cry. "I know it won't go on forever, but I don't have the strength to let him go. He would have to let me go."

Sure enough, two weeks later, he came to her cubicle full of excitement.

"Evette, guess what! Don't say anything, you are the first person that I am telling this to, but I have been offered a Summer Internship at an IT company in, get this, New York!"

Her insides collapsed. She knew it was God. She smiled anyway. "That's wonderful news, Anthony! I always knew you could do it."

"I will be leaving in five weeks."

"Wow." She said.

"What's the matter?" He asked.

"I may never see you again." She sadly said.

"Never say never because you never know." He smiled. "Things have a way of coming back around. I believe our paths will cross again." He lifted her head up with his fingers and said, "In the meantime, remember, Ma Ja-o. Don't fight."

AFTER

Saying Goodbye

In the weeks that followed, Anthony was so busy that they seldom saw each other. He was training another temporary staff person to take over his duties and they were trying to make sure that he got as much work out of the way as possible before he left. Evette had been moved to the 'other side' where all of the big wigs were and now shared an office with Dora and Tad. It had a wonderful view, so that made it bearable.

"I just wanted to let you know that this is my final week." Anthony came to her new 'office' and broke the news to her.

"Oh, really?" She responded.

"I brought you this." He held out a book and smiled. "I know you've never read one of his books, so I decided to give you one of my favorites."

It was a book written by Stephen King entitled 'The Shining.' Tears began to fill her eyes but she succeeded in holding them back.

"Thank you." Evette said as she received the book from him.

"Evette," he smiled, "that's another thing I admire about you."

"What's that?" She asked.

"You are always a lady. You always know how to maintain your composure." He took her hand, raised it and gently kissed it. She stood and he took her in his arms for one last hug, one last kiss.

"Just a little reminder. Something to remember me by." He whispered as she exhaled.

"There's nothing 'little' about you."

They both smiled as they slowly released each other.

"I'll miss you." She said.

"You speak as if we'll never see each other again."

"Well."

"Well, you should never say never because you never know." He cupped her face in his right hand. "Remember, finish your degree; achieve your goals and above all, Ma Ja-o. Don't fight. Promise?"

"I promise. Ma Ja-o."

After one last kiss on her cheek, he left the office and her life.

He was only in New York for a few months when it happened. The television in the conference room was on News Channel 2 when the reports came in. "A plane has crashed into one of the World Trade Center Towers in New York this morning. It's not sure if this is due to pilot error or.......Oh, my God! A second plane has just crashed into the second Tower. America is under attack! We're getting word that a third plane has crashed into the Pentagon. Oh, my God! Oh, my God! A fourth plane has crashed. It was determined that the fourth plane was headed for the White House. America has been attacked, ladies and gentlemen. America has been attacked. We will keep you informed as more information becomes available."

They were all fixated on the screen. They actually saw the second Tower get hit. Daniel's assistant slumped down in her chair like someone had punched her in the gut. She whispered, "Osama Bin Laden. He's the only one capable of something like this."

The date, ironically, was 9/11 and America was definitely in a state of emergency. Not since Pearl Harbor had any enemy of the US dared come onto its shores and attacked. Like any good enemy, though, Bin Laden knew that the best way to bring your rival down is not from without but from within. The terrorists had come here, were trained here, took flight lessons here, boarded and hi-jacked planes here! How could this have been allowed to happen? The perpetrators paid cash up front for their flight lessons. Had they been African American, they would have been arrested right then and the attacks would never have happened. But it did happen.

Across the screen, you could see people running, screaming, crying, trying to make their way through the debris that was falling from the sky and crashing around them. People were ashen from the dust and had an extreme look that was mingled with both horror and disbelief.

The most interesting thing about it was that everyone who was anyone was nowhere to be found. The president was somewhere reading a book (an upside down book); even the Vice President was not at the White House. All of the African Americans on the job knew instantly that they had knowledge of what was about to happen, but it would take a couple of years, and of course, a lot of tax payer's dollars before a Commission would be formed to tell everyone what blacks already knew - the government had been warned and failed to act.

Evette was devastated. With one plan of a demented man, someone she knew and loved was taken away. And for what, because someone felt that their god had told them to do so? Because someone didn't believe in freedom? Because someone hates the fact that America is everything that they are not allowed to be or are afraid to be?

They were all told that they could go home to their families. The schools closed down and Baltimore's mayor summoned all police to bunker down the inner harbor area. Baltimore's major ports, Trade Center and several other areas were presumed to be potential high targets. Barriers were put up in the down town area. It was like something out of a George Orwell novel. Evette was given a ride to her children's school because no one knew what the bus schedule was like.

"Thank you." Evette told her ride. "When we survive this, I'll buy you lunch."

"Girl, I'm only doing what Jesus would do. Go get your babies."

Evette ran up what now seemed to be an extremely long pathway to the school. She grabbed her children and ran home.

"Mommy what's wrong?" They asked.

"Everything is going to be okay. We just need to get home and pray."

"But why are you so scared?"

"Honestly?"

"Yes, mommy, please. You're scaring us?"

"Some very bad people have done some very bad things and we need to get home now and pray."

When she came through the door, she saw Alexander sitting on the couch watching television.

"You're home." He said.

She was livid. "I don't believe you are sitting here watching television. I'm sure you know that the schools had closed for the day. Why didn't you walk around the corner and get the children?"

"I figured you'd do it on your way home."

"You know what!" She took a deep breath and let it out slowly. "I'm going to give you what you have obviously wanted for a long time now."

"What's that?" He asked.

"A divorce."

"Okay." He said. "Let's talk about it."

"Alexander, whenever I disagreed with you on anything, you'd always throw divorce in my face as a means of shutting me up."

He started to open his mouth but she cut him off.

"Years before I messed up and you know I'm telling the truth. Now, I've finally decided to give you what you've been throwing in my face all these years."

He looked at her with a faint smile.

"It's about time. Evette, I never loved you. I didn't love you when I married you."

He thought his little confession would hurt her.

"Man, I've known from day one of this sham that you didn't love me because you never treated me as though you did. This is probably the first time you've ever been honest enough to admit what everyone has always known. So why did you ask me to marry you? Why go through all of this?"

"Evette, I married you for two reasons and two reasons only. Number one, for sex. I wanted to have all of my sexual fantasies fulfilled. Number two, because you have a powerful evangelistic anointing and I felt you'd be good to help grow my family's church. By the way, that whole thing with my brother was a set up and you were too dumb to see it. My brother and I have always shared everything. Ev-ver-y-thing. You didn't pay attention to the fact that I never made an effort, I mean I never even tried to please you until after it happened. You were too caught up in feeling guilty, which, of course, is what I knew you would do."

She interrupted. "I only have three questions for you. Who are you in love with? You owe me that much. Why didn't you marry that person? How much child support do you plan to pay?"

She stood there with her right hand on her hip and her right eyebrow raised, expecting a response.

"First of all, children are a consequence of sex. If you want anything from me, you'll have to get a court order to get it. Secondly, I didn't marry her because she said I wasn't worldly enough for her. I was, as she put it, too slow and inexperienced. Finally, she's my brother's wife."

Evette's head began to spin.

"You negros were wife swappin!"

"Yes. Well sort of. I swapped you but he hasn't swapped her yet."

"So it appears that the real jackass in the situation is you."

"No, Evette. That would be you. See, your Pastor tried to warn you, but you wouldn't listen. I even tried to force you to leave but you wouldn't. You're so damn stubborn."

"Tried to force me to leave. How? When?"

"The house. The car. Not working consistently and forcing you to take on all the pressures yourself. Any decent, self-respecting woman would have left, but not you. Your pride was too strong. So, now go. I'll see the kids every first and third Saturday from noon to four."

"Eight hours a month? Oh, hell naw you won't. You'll have your children at least every first and third weekend. You will never be able to tell people that I've kept you away from your children."

"Whatever. What are you doing?"

Evette was at the computer typing up a statement. It was only one paragraph. She printed it.

"Sign it and date it." She demanded.

"What's this?"

"It's just a statement of intent. It says that we both agree, today, that we're separating for purposes of a divorce. It also states how much you agree to pay in child support."

"Okay. Fine." He signed and dated it. Then she did the same. She'd put his name first, giving it the appearance of having been his idea.

Three weeks later, he came home from work and discovered that she and the children were moving out. He helped them.

The Set Up Begins

The phone rang.

"Hello."

"May I speak to Sis. Evette Worthington, please?"

It was Lonnie. He was an ordained elder at a newly formed church in Delaware.

"How'd you get my number?" Evette asked.

"I guess you forgot that you're listed. I dialed 4-1-1."

"Oh. Duh! I feel really stupid right about now. So, how ya doin'? It's been a long time."

"I've been kool. Working on some stuff. Look, I heard about you and Alexander. How're you adjusting to being a single mom?"

"I'm sure everyone has head by now. I'm hangin' in there."

"You know, Evette, I've been thinking about you a lot lately."

"Really?" She questioned sarcastically.

"Are you surprised?"

"Yes."

"You were quite a homely lookin' thing when we were all in church together years ago."

"If this is your way of being charming, you need to return to charm school and get a refund."

"No, no. I'm not trying to offend you. It's just that back then, you looked so, so plain-Jane. I always pictured what you'd look like with makeup and stylish clothes that fit."

"Again. Where is the charming part? When is it going to kick in?"

They both laughed.

"Evette, what I'm trying to say is that I have always thought you were beautiful and wondered how much more you could've been if Alexander had taken care of you. I can still see those beautiful cat-eyes of yours and your skin.... Hmmm. Soft looking and golden brown. Passionate as a luscious peach. Do you mind if I call you that?"

"What?" She asked.

"Passion. Do you mind if I call you Passion?"

No, I don't mind. I think it's kinda cute."

"Great. You're my Passion."

"I belong to no one."

"So I've been told."

"What's that supposed to mean?"

"It means that women like you can only belong to certain types of men."

"And what 'type' would you say that is?"

"The type that understands how to satisfy your mind before he can appreciate your body. The kind that can caress and stimulate the intelligent, creative side of you. That can tap into your spiritual anointing. That's the only kind of man that can handle you. Anyone less than that is undeserving of you."

"So, you think you know me, huh?"

"No. I don't know you, but I do know your type."

"And what type would that be?"

"Creative."

"Creative?" Evette asked.

"Yes, creative. That sums up everything about you, Passion."

"Really now? Does it really? Don't tell me. You've popped into my life to 'explore' my creative side." She stated more than asked.

"Passion, there's a depth to you that you haven't even tapped into yet. Believe me, you haven't scratched the surface."

"Well, Lonnie, I have to go. I'm sure we'll talk again. Take care."

"Yeah. I'll call you later on tonight."

"No. I have to be somewhere."

"Where are you going after 9 o'clock on a Wednesday night?"

"This spot on Guilford Avenue. I was told that they have open-mic every Wednesday night. I'm going there to read a couple of my poems."

"Do your thing. What's your stage name?"

"I think I'll use Passion."

"Okay, Ms. Passion. Call me when you get back and let me know how it went."

"Okay. Talk to you later."

"Bye."

She blurted before he hung up. "Lonnie!"

"Yes?"

"Never say goodbye."

"Why?" He asked.

"Because goodbye is forever."

"Okay, then. Talk to you later."

She smiled. "Lonnie."

"Yes, Passion?"

"One more thing. Repeat after me. Say game…"

"Game"

"Tight"

"Tight. Girl, you're crazy."

"Talk to you later." She hung up.

****

"Are you there?" Lonnie asked.

"Yeah. I'm here."

"What do you think?"

"She sounds sweet. Deeply wounded, but sweet. You don't' wanna damage her anymore than she has been, Lonnie."

"But how do I get to her?"

"The same way you said. Her intellect. If you come straight out and chase her, she'll only run away. Hunt her. Slow walk her down. Think ten steps ahead of her."

"I thought in Chess, you think five moves ahead of your opponent?"

"Yes, but this isn't Chess. This is Evette and she's a thinker. Trust me, she's already five moves ahead of you."

"So, what do I do?"

"Treat her the way a woman usually does a man."

"What? What's that supposed to mean?"

"Make her think it was her idea. Take the passive, accommodating role. Make subtle suggestions that her mind will pick up, meditate on and regurgitate back to you as if she thought about it on her own. Make her think it's all her doing - that YOU are the one being taken on HER ride. HER fantasy. HER hidden passions. Understand?"

"I understand."

"By the way, I like that Passion thing you came up with. She'll begin to identify that as her alter ego"

"I AM the man."

"Call me after she calls you."

"Kool."

At New Seasons on Guilford Avenue, "Ladies and gentlemen, we have a virgin in the house. So be gentle." Laughter.

Evette got up and approached the mic. "Let's give a warm New Seasons welcome." Applause. "Everybody, let's get a taste of Passion!"